Capitalism

versus

Socialism

What Does the Bible Have to Say?

Thomas D. Simpson, Ph.D.

Cover design by 100Covers.com
Formatted by FormattedBooks.com

ISBN: 978-1-7348156-0-3

Dedication

This book is dedicated to my friend, partner, soul mate, and wife, Cindy, who has encouraged and supported me throughout this book-writing venture.

"Those who do not remember the past are condemned to repeat it."

—GEORGE SANTAYANA

Contents

Preface

One of the more startling developments of recent years has been a renewed enthusiasm for socialism, especially among millennials and Generation Z. Indeed, opinion polls show that American millennials and Generation Zers have a highly favorable attitude toward socialism. Polls indicate that upwards of 70 percent of people in these age groups favor socialism. They perceive that socialism provides more economic security, a greater sense of togetherness, and more equality of wealth and income. Adding to the popularity of socialism is an underlying notion that, under socialism, the things we want—college education, health care, and housing—would be free of charge. There's very little realization that these things require costly resources and must, at the end of the day, be paid for. In other words, to get these things for free, ultimately, we have to give up other things—indeed, a lot of these other things—that we also value.

Very seldom do you hear proponents of socialism addressing the other side of the coin: What the average person must give up to get these "freebies." And how, in the end, it will be impossible to satisfy everybody's wants. Invariably, there will be some type of unpopular rationing procedure to determine who the lucky ones are who get the scarce items being provided for free. Moreover, these rationing procedures inevitably pose an irresistible temptation for corruption. Those deciding who actually gets the scarce item can line their pockets with surreptitious payments from those most wanting it. It happens all the time.

Overlooked, too, is the tendency for such centrally directed economic systems to override personal freedom. When the government makes choices for us, we have ceded our right to make those choices ourselves. And the more choices that we've turned over to the government, the more our personal freedom has been curtailed.

Also playing a role is an attitude that has developed— aided by the media and Hollywood—that our market-based (capitalistic) system is based on greed, exploitation, and abuse. It's a rigged system in which the average person doesn't have a chance.

In addition to being unfair and drawing out the worst in people, inherent in capitalism are financial crises and major economic disruptions. Indeed, the financial crisis and Great Recession of 2008 and 2009 played an indisputable role in fostering these attitudes. Capitalism is portrayed as a dog-eat-dog system in which only the fittest and craftiest survive. This can be pretty scary, especially for those who have always gotten a shiny trophy for participating in competitive events, regardless of where they finished. The popularity of Bernie Sanders and, more recently, Alexandria Ocasio-Cortez (AOC) epitomizes the attraction of millennials and Gen Z to socialism.

Meanwhile, Che Guevara, associated with Marxist revolutionary movements in the Western Hemisphere, is lionized as a champion of the downtrodden. Che is commonly found on tee shirts of the young. Lost in all of this is the historical record of the real Che. The real Che was ruthless in his dealings with anyone who opposed him. He was responsible for the murder of thousands and he fiercely beat thousands more.

The popularity of socialism seems ironic in light of the long trail of failures of socialism in its various forms, including pervasive corruption and brutal suppression of opponents. Moreover, we can watch a real-time example in Venezuela, which has been disintegrating before our very eyes—empty shelves, ongoing electrical blackouts, vanishing health care, historic hyperinflation, government repression, widespread corruption, and murders of families seeking to escape across its borders. Or contrast North and South Korea—the former a communist (socialist) system and the latter a capitalist (or market-based) system. The people who live in these countries share the same cultural heritage and inhabit the same corner of the earth. Yet one group perpetually lives at the edge of starvation and is subjugated by a vicious regime while the other—which may have produced your car, TV, or smart phone—thrives.

These examples reveal a huge chasm between the utopian ideals of socialist thinkers and actual performance. Interestingly, those countries that had been socialist in Eastern Europe have embraced market principles and have no desire to return. Nonetheless, Bernie's views on the desirability of socialism have changed little over the decades, even in the face of the lengthy string of failures. The examples also reveal a widespread jaundiced view of the contributions of market (capitalist) systems, which have done more to raise standards of living around the world and lift people out of poverty than any other economic system in history.

This fascination with socialism by millennials and Gen Z is another example of the validity of George Santayana's statement that "Those who don't remember the past are condemned to repeat it."

Yet many have argued that socialism is most consistent with biblical teachings. Frequently mentioned is the early church in Jerusalem described in Acts 2:42-47. Believers were selling their possessions and sharing with others, so that the needs of each member of that community were being met. Also, other biblical references to caring for the poor and the curse of being rich are viewed as supporting a system in which government performs the role of the leveler—redistributing wealth from the rich to the poor.

This book addresses the fundamental features of all major economic systems, including capitalist and socialist systems. Communism is a variety of a socialist system, and fascist systems—most notably those of Nazi Germany and Fascist Italy—have their origins in socialism. These are contrasted with the basic features of a capitalist or market-based system. The Bible doesn't prescribe any specific economic system but is fairly clear about the underpinnings—or pillars—of these economic systems.

This book uses the term "market-based" system instead of "capitalist" system. The latter has more emotive content and is misleading. Karl Marx, author of the *Communist Manifesto* and *Das Kapital,* favored the term "capitalist," and the term is widely used today by critics of market-based systems. Marx saw the population as divided into two opposing groups—workers and capitalists. Capitalists were the owners of the businesses that employed the workers and of the capital or machines used by workers in the production process. Marx described worker-employer relationships in the context of the manufacturing sector, in which employers were factory owners.

In his view, a highly adversarial relationship existed between workers and capitalists, one in which capitalists had the upper hand and routinely exploited their workers in their pursuit of greed. Capitalists expropriated for themselves some of the value created by workers during the production process—value that legitimately belonged to workers. Moreover, one's economic and social position was passed along to the next generation; thus, your economic and social plight was determined by your birth. The offspring of capitalists became the next generation of owners and managers of factories while the offspring of workers became the next generation of exploited workers. For the workers, there were no avenues of upward mobility for their children—their children, too, were stuck in the misery foisted on them by greedy and uncaring capitalists. Furthermore, workers and capitalists formed the primary social classes, and tension between the two also represented a grave social clash.

This was a highly simplified characterization of economic reality, even in Marx's day. It didn't describe agricultural, retail, and other service workers who were around in large numbers at the time of Marx's writings. In these sectors of the economy, family operations, sole proprietorships, and partnerships were common. In these situations, relationships between owners and those providing labor were typically much different.

Today, we live in an economy that's largely a service economy, in which more than two-thirds of total output takes the form of services instead of manufactured, tangible goods. More importantly, modern employers—be they in the service sector or manufacturing—realize that satisfied employees are more productive and more valuable to the company than disgruntled workers. Furthermore, in a competitive labor market, discontented workers can leave and are prone to search for greener pastures. When this occurs, employers must undertake costly searches for replacements and costly training programs for new hires, not to mention disruptions to the production process while this is taking place. In response, we see employers luring new workers and seeking to retain existing workers by offering flex-hours, work-from-home, and other amenities that cater to changing lifestyles, along with competitive compensation. In these circumstances, workers in the private sector today see very little need for labor unions to represent them in dealing with conflicts with their employers, as witnessed by a paltry 6% of the private sector labor force being unionized.

Consequently, the differences between workers and employers have become blurred. Workers own corporations through their 401(k) plans and through their savings placed in mutual funds. In that sense, they're capitalists. And managers of many successful businesses place their desks out with their employees, dress like them, and mingle with them throughout the working day. Business managers do have some ownership in the businesses they manage, but this typically is required by the board of directors chosen by the shareholders and to whom managers are accountable. The board wants its managers to have "skin in the game" to better align the managers' interests with those of the other shareholders, so that their actions will be in the best interest of shareholders generally.

Moreover, those with the greatest holdings of wealth today haven't acquired that wealth through inheritance. The wealthiest today are self-made entrepreneurs. In other words, the wealthiest Americans have created their own wealth and haven't had it passed down to them. The top ten wealthiest Americans have names such as Gates, Zuckerberg, Bloomberg, Koch, and Brin—one of these is barely into his thirties. They're all multi-billionaires. Some made their fortune by translating a novel idea into a product used widely around the globe, while others used keen judgment to find established businesses that were languishing and needed help to turn their fortunes around.

For these reasons, the term "market-based" is used instead of the term "capitalist" to refer to a system in which people—be they employees or employers, consumers or businesses—respond to market incentives as they pursue their self-interest. In this setting, economic outcomes result from the interactions of these numerous parties, each pursuing their self-interest—and not from central plans and direction. Property is privately owned, and large numbers of workers also have an ownership stake in corporate businesses, often indirectly through 401(k)s and other retirement plans. In the appendix, we'll examine the conditions that are required for such an economic system to perform at a high level and get the most out of the resources available.

It's worth noting that many of the proponents of socialism today appear to have a somewhat different version in mind than the types of socialism that have described the past. Under standard forms of socialism, property is owned collectively—and not privately. Production takes place through state- or collectively owned enterprises, not through private businesses. Socialists today focus more on using the state to redistribute income and wealth and to make widely available certain goods and services to the public, such as health care and higher education, at no out-of-pocket cost. Some see production being undertaken by government while others see a role for private suppliers. In any event, the government would be applying a heavy hand in regulating and controlling the economy, as in more traditional socialist and fascist systems. As a consequence, the scope for corruption and abuse is magnified, as in those other non-market systems.

In practice, most economies today are, in varying degrees, welfare states, relying on market forces for the bulk of the production of goods and services and the government to provide a safety net to those at the lower end of the income spectrum. The resources for the safety net come from disproportionately high taxes on those at the upper end. The United States has introduced a moderate welfare state, while Northern European countries have gone considerably further.

As noted, the Bible doesn't specifically prescribe any of the economic systems addressed here, those that have characterized the past century. However, each of these systems is built on four pillars, and the Bible does have something to say on these. Perhaps, not too surprisingly, the Bible is most consistent with the system that the nation's founders established, one based on freedom and individual choice.

This book is an outgrowth of an invitation that I received to speak on alternative economic systems—communism, socialism, and capitalism—including which is most compatible with biblical teachings at an annual Ratio Christi Symposium. As I researched the topic, it became clearer to me that market-based systems are most consistent with the teachings of the Bible.

Nonetheless, the Bible doesn't condone excesses that can develop in a market economy (or any other economy), and each of us has a responsibility to care for those unable to care for themselves and to resist the temptation for wealth to become an obsession in our lives and stand above God.

By way of background, my appreciation for the basic workings of market-based economic systems has grown over a lifetime of being a student of economics and economic systems. I was raised the son of parents who struggled to make ends meet during the Depression of the 1930s, and who regarded government and labor unions to be a necessary protector of workers and consumers. Indeed, my father served as president of a labor union for a number of years. Needless to say, my parents were skeptical of free and open markets. Growing up, I also had the view that private business activity—working for businesses or buying from some businesses—was tainted. There was something morally questionable about doing so. Government and nonprofit organizations were more virtuous.

However, once I began studying economics in college, my views started to change. I began developing a realization that market-based systems are complex ecosystems that work in harmony to deliver impressive results. Also, I came to realize that people pursuing self-interest in the marketplace isn't much different than pursuing self-interest by eating when feeling hungry. We are wired this way to preserve life by an intelligent designer. This appreciation for market systems grew as a Ph.D. student in economics at the University of Chicago. The contrast between economic performance under market-based and socialist and communist regimes took on new meaning during my career as a central banker at the Federal Reserve Board in

Washington, D.C. In that capacity, I was privileged to be able to provide technical assistance to central banks in former socialist and communist systems. These nations had lived with the widespread shortcomings of centrally directed economies and wanted to emulate the performance of the United States and other market economies. Moreover, at the same time, most also were turning to democracy as a way of enabling their citizens to choose their political leaders and how they would be governed, in keeping with their new freedom to choose what to buy in the marketplace and where to work.

The vibrancy of economic life in well-functioning market systems is palpable. Moreover, these systems, perhaps ironically, treat individuals with more basic dignity, and are more compatible with democratic political systems than the others. They provide more transparency and less scope for corruption than other systems. But they're not perfect and come with a list of well-known market failures. In those circumstances, they provide opportunities for humans to use their God-given abilities to develop public policy to achieve better outcomes, although it needs to be noted that the cure for the shortcomings can sometimes be worse than the disease. This is to say that all economic systems, including market-based systems, come short of delivering perfection—which is the human condition in a fallen world. It will continue to be the human condition until, as the Bible assures us, Christ returns.

This book is written for all persons interested in the issue of capitalism versus socialism and wanting an authoritative and even-handed treatment of the topic. It's written for an audience having no background in economics. It's especially of value to parents who want their children to be well informed on this critical issue. Indeed, each chapter has some questions to stimulate good discussion around the dinner table. They're intended to launch a constructive back and forth discussion and not necessarily to come up with definitive answers.

A few biblical propositions underlie the arguments presented in this book:

- The Bible from Genesis through Revelation is the revealed word of God and is to be relied upon and trusted in making decisions and forming judgments.

- God created humans in His image, including giving us the ability to reason and the opportunity to make our own decisions (Genesis 2). This implies that all humans have immense value, and that no one person is any more important than any other. It also implies that individuals are competent to make important decisions.

- In exercising our freedom to make decisions, we have repeatedly chosen to put our will ahead of God's (Genesis 3—committed sin). The consequence has been a fallen (imperfect) world. A just God cannot tolerate sin and relegates all of us sinners to an eternity apart from Him—hell.

- But God is also a loving God who has provided a plan for redemption, through His son, Jesus. Jesus ushered in a new era (kingdom of God) for those who accept Him and his sacrifice. He will return at some undisclosed time in the future to restore creation (Daniel and Revelation). Perfection won't come until then. In the meantime, we'll remain consigned to a fallen world, but one that we can and are obligated to make better.

CHAPTER 1

Pillars of Economic Systems

BACKGROUND

Is it true that the Bible supports socialism? Aren't socialist systems more compassionate, fair, and equitable, in line with the teachings of Christ? Surely, the early Christian community described in Acts Chapters 2 and 4 was intended to be a model for us and our economy, wasn't it?

In Acts 2: 44-47 we are told: "And all who believed were together and had all things in common. And they were selling their possessions and belongings and distributing the proceeds to all, as any had need. And day by day, attending the temple together and breaking bread in their homes, they received their food with glad and generous hearts, praising God and having favor with all the people. And the Lord added to their number day by day those who were being saved."[1] This is followed in Acts 4:32 by "Now the full number of those who believed were of one heart and soul, and no one said that any of the things that belonged to him was his own, but they had everything in common."

Moreover, there's no shortage of passages in the Bible that stress the importance of caring for the poor, the widows, and the sojourners. Also, the Bible has numerous passages that are critical of those with great wealth. Notably, we need to go no farther than to the encounter between Jesus and the rich young ruler described in Matthew 19. This young man wanted to know what he had to do to gain eternal life. After responding to Jesus by telling him that he had kept the fifth through tenth commandments, Jesus said in verse 21, "If you would be perfect, go, sell what you possess and give to the poor, and you will have treasure in heaven." Certainly, this must give support to the government taking an active role in redistributing wealth from the rich to the poor.

THE PILLARS OF AN ECONOMIC SYSTEM

Not so fast! This is a selective and superficial reading of what the Bible has to say on economics. We need to dig deeper and wider. A good place to start is finding out what the Bible has to say about the underlying pillars of any economic system. The

---

1   *The Holy Bible: English Standard Version.* (2016). Wheaton: Standard Bible Society. Biblical quotations in this book are from the English Standard Version.

answers to the following questions serve as the foundation of any economic system, whether it's market-based (capitalist), socialist, or something else: Who owns property—be it for personal or productive use? Who decides what gets produced? Who decides how it gets produced? And how are the things that get produced distributed among members of the population (income distribution)? Capitalist and socialist systems differ greatly on the answers to these questions.

CLASSIFICATION CRITERIA

To investigate the alternative economic systems, we address the four criteria mentioned above. These are shown in the table below (note that communism is regarded as a variant of socialism):

	Property ownership	What is produced?	How is it produced?	How is output distributed?
Socialism/ Communism	State	State	State	State
Fascism	Private	State	Private	State/private
Market	Private	Private	Private	Private

Socialism. In a socialist system, property is collectively owned. It can be thought of as owned by the state on behalf of all of its citizens. Decisions regarding what gets produced are made by a body that represents the collective—a state-planning agency. That agency also has responsibility for deciding how each item gets produced—and allocates inputs in the form of labor and other resources to each entity responsible for production. Distribution is made by the collective entity based on some norm—which could be equality or fairness (based on some notion of fairness) or it could be based on rewarding those who advance other goals of the state (such as prestige from winning global competition in an athletic event or chess).

Communism. Communism is a form of socialism. It's based on an ideology largely developed by Karl Marx—and his frequent collaborator, Frederick Engels. That ideology envisions the state owning property on behalf of its citizens and utilizing a central planning agency to decide what to produce, how to produce it, and how it's to be distributed. But Marx also envisioned that in time the state would wither away as it would no longer be necessary for achieving the goals of an idyllic society. In his utopian world, individuals would be completely transformed and would be motivated by the interest of the collective instead of self-interest. They would willingly share property, produce those goods and services that they believed would contribute the most to the public as a whole, and take for themselves only what they needed. All members of this society somehow would work in harmony and there would be enough for everybody.

Fascism. Fascism (including Nazism of Hitler's Germany) is also an offshoot of socialism. Indeed, the term "Nazism" is a contraction of National Socialism. Fascism differs from the socialist systems already mentioned in that property is mostly privately owned. However, owners of property are not free to use their property as they wish but are directed by the state. Like other forms of socialism, production is centrally directed by a state planning authority. Industry cartels are formed among producers in a sector, with product lines and production levels established by the state-planning agency. Wages and prices are also set by the planning agency, not by market forces, and "excess income" is expropriated by the state. Fascist systems also have been extremely nationalistic and are noted for espousing intense racial and ethnic superiority.

Many advocates of socialism today—such as Bernie and AOC—actually seem to favor something more akin to fascism. They advocate a highly taxed and highly regulated economy but haven't made a big pitch for widespread state ownership of property.

Market-based systems. In a market-based system, property is privately owned. Individuals make decisions based on their self-interest—as consumers and as workers, providers of labor services. Businesses make decisions based on their self-interest as producers of goods and services and as employers. It's a bottoms-up system unlike the others that are top-down. When there are few restrictions placed on market participants, the outcomes in a wide variety of circumstances are as follows: the items that get produced are the items that consumers want; they're produced in the amounts people want; and they're produced at the lowest costs and prices. While these outcomes prevail over a wide variety of situations, in certain circumstances, market-based systems come short of achieving these results, leaving scope for government to step in for a better result. This can include the government playing a role in redistribution.

Welfare states. It should be noted that some countries, such as the Nordic countries, notably Sweden, are said to be socialist systems. However, they permit widespread ownership of property, and property owners have considerable freedom in how they use their property. They have privately owned businesses that are highly competitive and permit individuals to own their homes, cars, and other personal property. These systems attempt to use public policy to change the distribution of income by taxing persons, especially those with higher incomes, heavily and using the tax proceeds to provide various services, such as health care and postsecondary education, at little or no cost. They have created an elaborate safety net for their citizens that covers substantial losses that occur when there's a serious illness or loss of a job. According to our classification scheme, such countries fall into the market-based category. They rely on private property and market forces to determine what gets produced and how it gets produced, but the state plays a big role in distribution.

These days, all market-based systems are involved in some form of redistribution—transferring from the rich to the poor—and the differences among economies are a matter of degree. It's worth noting that public policies focused on redistribution, such as graduated income taxes, affect incentives and reduce efficiency—shrink the size of the overall pie. This will be discussed in more detail in Chapter 5 on the welfare state.

Some welfare states, such as Great Britain, also turned to nationalization of various industries. Included were coal, steel, rail, and telecommunications. However, they discovered after decades of disappointing experience, that state ownership and control resulted in huge inefficiencies in these sectors. As a consequence, they chose to reverse this through privatization (selling off) of many of these industries and turned to more reliance on market forces.

THE ROAD AHEAD

In the chapters that follow, we'll look at market-based economies first. Market-based systems follow well-articulated principles and serve as a useful framework and benchmark for understanding other systems. Those principles are developed in greater detail in the appendix. A chapter examining socialism follows the chapter on market-based systems. Following this is a chapter dealing with communism and fascism. Then we explore welfare states. The epilogue sums things up.

But before we look at the different economic systems, we'll delve into what the Bible has to say about the four pillars that we listed above. It should be noted that the Bible doesn't specifically prescribe any of the economic systems introduced above. Nonetheless, there are certain conclusions that we can reach from Scripture that can help guide us to an understanding of which system is most consistent with biblical teaching.

WHAT DOES THE BIBLE HAVE TO SAY?

Collective ownership. In a fundamental sense, all property belongs to God, the Creator. However, as described in Genesis 1:28, God delegated responsibility to subdue the earth and gave dominion over living creatures to humans.

The portions of the book of Acts mentioned at the beginning of this chapter might be viewed as supporting collective ownership of property, as in a socialist system. Acts 2, 4, and 5 describe how some of the early Christian believers in Jesus, being filled with the Holy Spirit, sold their possessions and pooled the proceeds. From these common resources, the economic needs of each member of the community were satisfied

These were euphoric times and a strong sense of community and caring for each member of the community prevailed among followers of Christ. The love of Christ as seen in John 13:34-35 was clearly evident in this community: "A new commandment I give to you, that you love one another: just as I have loved you, you also are to love one another. By this all people will know that you are my disciples, if you have love for one another."

Acts 4 suggests that this sharing of property continued for a time. This chapter notes that considerable grace was upon this community and there wasn't one needy person among them. Moreover, Chapter 5 describes a tragic outcome for two members of that community—Ananias and his wife, Sapphira—who sold a piece of property and held back some of the proceeds. Both of them died suddenly, presumably as a consequence of lying about whether they had turned over all of the proceeds to the apostles for the well-being of the community. It could be inferred from these verses that there are pretty severe consequences for not sharing all of what they received from the sale of the property. But Peter accused Ananias of lying to God before Ananias fell dead. This suggests that lying was principally behind Ananias and his wife's fate, not so much the hoarding of some of the proceeds from the sale for their personal use.

It's noteworthy that members of this community gave up their personal property to share with others voluntarily—indeed, cheerfully. Coercion isn't suggested. Thus, these passages, by themselves, cannot be viewed as justifying the compelling of the haves to provide for the have-nots, as occurs through government programs today that tax the many to provide for the less well off.

Instead, they call for a caring attitude toward the well-being of others—a point emphasized repeatedly throughout Scripture. God is pleased when we willfully—and cheerfully—respond to the needs of the less fortunate. Moreover, this type of communal living and sharing arrangement isn't prescribed by the apostle Paul or other authors elsewhere in the New Testament. Indeed, some biblical commentators believe that this early church experience is to be viewed as a foretaste of what to expect in the millennial kingdom, once the Messiah returns.

Private Ownership. Possessions often are treated in Scripture as a gift or blessing from God to an individual. In Psalm 112:1-3, we are told that "Blessed is the man who fears the LORD, who greatly delights in his commandments....Wealth and riches are in his house,…" In Genesis, we learn that Abraham had great wealth and God blessed his son, Isaac, with great wealth. Similarly, God blessed Isaac's son, Jacob, with considerable wealth, especially in the wake of efforts by his father-in-law to cheat him out of possessions. Elsewhere, Job was given double his possessions after his lengthy and painful testing, as a blessing from God.

This shouldn't be seen as the so-called prosperity gospel in which, if one has faith in God and does certain things, they'll be blessed with wealth. According to this way of thinking, the end is wealth and the means of getting it is God. But we know from Scripture, including the first four of the Ten Commandments (Exodus, Chapter 20), that God is to be the end. It should also be recognized that even when God is the end, the person might not be blessed with wealth. Indeed, the person may face considerable hardship. A sovereign God is free to choose how each believer is to be treated, and an omniscient God knows what's eternally in our best interest. The only promise for the believer who puts God first is that they'll receive a peace (shalom) that passes all understanding through a personal relationship with the Creator and will come out of suffering a stronger and more God-trusting person.

Moreover, God was very explicit about inheritance of property, specifying how property was to be passed down from one generation to the next. This is spelled out in Deuteronomy 21:15-17 and Numbers 27:8-11. These verses specify how property was to be passed along from a father to his sons or, if no sons, to his daughter, or, if no daughter, to his brothers, and so forth. Clearly, this presupposes private ownership of property.

Thus, Scripture is pretty clear in indicating that God condones private ownership of property. Moreover, God seems to be okay with some people holding large amounts of wealth; indeed, as noted above, we are told that God blessed some individuals with vast amounts of wealth.

Other commandments from the Ten Commandments confirm that people are allowed to own property—and property rights are to be respected and taken seriously. The eighth commandment tells us that we are not to steal from our neighbor. Moreover, the tenth commandment instructs us not to covet those things belonging to our neighbor—home, animals, or anything else that's owned by our neighbor. This clearly instructs us to respect the right of our neighbor to their property and to be content with what we have. Chapters 21 and 22 of Exodus go into considerable detail about restitution when property rights have been violated.

Elsewhere, the Bible established the rule of tithing (Deuteronomy 14). This presumes that people are to own property and that a tenth of the fruits from that property is to be returned to God. As a sidelight, elsewhere, the Bible prescribes that the portion given to God is to be the best tenth. Proverbs 3: 9-10, tell us, "Honor the LORD with your wealth and with the first fruits of your produce, then your barns will be filled with plenty...." God wants us to regard Him as our top priority. When we place Him as our top priority, blessings flow. Those blessings may take the form of wealth or they may take other forms. In all cases, the follower experiences shalom, true peace and contentment, regardless of the circumstances.

The Capacity of Individuals as Consumers and Workers. A key issue in the compatibility of the various economic systems with the Bible is the fundamental nature of humans. Does the individual have the capacity to make decisions that promote their own well-being? If so, we can trust individuals to make sound economic decisions regarding what they buy and consume and what kind of work they do. If not, then there perhaps are others who are in a better position to make those decisions for them. Also, when individuals make their own decisions, what are the consequences for others? Do others benefit or are they disadvantaged?

The Bible in Genesis 1:26 -28 tells us:
[26] Then God said, "Let us make man in our image, after our likeness. And let them have dominion over the fish of the sea and over the birds of the heavens and over the livestock and over all the earth and over every creeping thing that creeps on the earth. [27] So God created man in his own image, in the image of God he created him; male and female he created them. [28] And God

blessed them. And God said to them, 'Be fruitful and multiply and fill the earth and subdue it, and have dominion over the fish of the sea and over the birds of the heavens and over every living thing that moves on the earth.'"

These verses imply that God created humans with the capacity to reason and make good decisions. After all, He charges humans with the responsibility to subdue His earthly creation and to have dominion over other living creatures. Managing such a project properly clearly requires intelligence, knowledge, sound reasoning skills, and keen judgment. Nowhere in Scripture is it mentioned that only a select few have these abilities and, thus, should be given responsibility for making decisions for others. Moreover, He calls on each individual to make the most important decision in their life: The decision of whether to accept the gift of eternal salvation or not. No one else can make that decision for us. All of this tells us that individuals are capable of making economic decisions that bear on their well-being. Thus, the Bible seems to be okay with individuals making their own decisions in the marketplace regarding what they will buy and consume and what kind of work they will do and who they will work for.

To be able to address the issue of whether economic decisions made by individuals are beneficial or detrimental to others, we need to be able to see how the pursuit of self-interest by an individual interacts with the pursuit of self-interest by others and whether the final result is that others are better off or not. If the size of the economic pie (the total amount of goods and services) is unchanged, then one individual will gain at the expense of others. It's a zero-sum game. But, if the pie can expand or contract, then the pursuit of self-interest by an individual may lead to the pie expanding sufficiently that not only is this individual better off but others are better off, as well. We will see in the next chapter that this is a fundamental feature of a market-based economy and has been recognized for nearly two and a half centuries.

Enabling individuals to be free to make economic choices, a fundamental principle underlying market-based economies, naturally extends to individuals making political decisions in the form of self-governance—democracy. Both political and economic freedom are an outgrowth of the Enlightenment movement of the eighteenth century in which humans are seen to be endowed with the God-given capacity to reason and use that capacity to self-govern and to improve their lot in the marketplace. Interestingly, this capacity of individuals was also seen to improve knowledge and well-being through free scientific discovery. Such freedom was captured in the U.S. Declaration of Independence, which referred to the Creator as endowing individuals with certain unalienable rights—namely, to life, liberty, and the pursuit of happiness. Enlightenment thinking can be traced back to Martin Luther and the Reformation. In this movement, all individuals were believed to have the capacity to read and understand the Bible, allowing them to develop a personal relationship directly with God without relying on an intermediary. In view of these considerations, it's not surprising that political democracies and market-based economies typically go together.

The Capacity of Individual Producers. Much the same can be said about individuals who manage businesses that produce goods and services for others and utilize valuable resources in the process. The Bible doesn't suggest that only a few elites have this capacity and, thus, production decisions, such as what to produce and how to produce it, should be reserved just for them. Jesus' disciples were ordinary fisherman, but they made their own decisions about when and where to fish and to whom to sell their catch. Jesus told parables about private farm owners who exercised their own discretion in what they produced and whom they employed. In other words, one cannot find passages in Scripture that point to a collective decision process for production of goods and services.

Distribution: The Poor and the Rich. In contrast, the Bible does have a lot to say about the poor and about the responsibility of the wealthy. The Bible is replete with passages that illustrate God's concern for the poor—those unable to provide sufficiently for their own well-being.[2] Very often, these are people who don't own land that can be used to provide for their needs. In Deuteronomy 15:11, God says, "For there will never cease to be poor in the land. Therefore, I command you, you shall open wide your hand to your brother, to the needy, and to the poor,

---

2   One might ask why God wants us to share with the poor. Is He unable to come up with the resources to provide for them Himself and needs us to help Him out? This looks pretty preposterous when we consider that we are talking about God, the creator of the vast universe. Surely, He can create a little more to ensure that the needs of the less fortunate are met. Since He has chosen not to do so, we can infer that God wants us individually to show that we value our relationship with Him enough to want to please Him by being obedient and by sacrificing from what we have to provide for the needs of others. It seems likely that God is telling us that the sacrifice we make for others is not only good for them, but it also is good for us.

in your land." In Exodus 23:11, God instructs the people of Israel each seventh year not to plow their tracts of land so that the poor can get food from them.[3] In Leviticus 19:9-10, God tells Moses that the people of Israel were not to harvest the edges of their fields and were to leave the gleanings for the poor. In Psalm 41, King David says, "Blessed is the one who considers the poor! In the day of trouble, the LORD delivers him; the LORD protects him and keeps him alive…." In Proverbs 21:13, it says "Whoever closes his ear to the cry of the poor will himself call out and not be answered." In the New Testament, God's heart for the poor is expressed by Jesus in Luke 6:20 "Blessed are you who are poor, for yours is the kingdom of God."

It's noteworthy that, while exhorting us to care for the poor, Jesus tells us that the poor will always be with us. In Matthew 26:11, in response to the disciple's criticism of Mary, the sister of Martha and Lazarus, for pouring expensive ointment over him, Jesus said "For you will always have the poor with you, but you won't always have me." This echoes the passage in Deuteronomy 15:11 mentioned above. The statement by Jesus affirms Mary's priorities of spending a small fortune on precious oil to anoint Jesus' body for His forthcoming burial that was to be a part of the series of events that would provide eternal salvation for the many instead of temporary relief for just a few. Moreover, it tells us that each generation will be faced with the challenge of heeding God's commandment to honor Him by caring for the

---

3   So serious was God about His command regarding keeping the sabbatical, that this was an important reason behind His punishment of the Jewish people through the exile to Assyria and Babylon. They were required to complete seventy sabbatical years in exile, each corresponding to a sabbatical year that they missed while inhabiting the land of Israel.

poor. It further implies that the utopian ideal of vanquishing poverty won't be achieved until this age has come to a close.

Also, biblical injunctions to care for the poor address this as an individual's responsibility and don't mention that it's a collective responsibility through a governing body—the state. We please God as individuals by caring for the needs of the poor and others whom He loves and by doing this out of love cheerfully. Paul, in 2 Corinthians 9:7-9, says "Each one must give as he has decided in his heart, not reluctantly or under compulsion, for God loves a cheerful giver. And God is able to make all grace abound in you, so that having sufficiency in all things at all times, you may abound in every good work. As it is written, 'He has distributed freely, he has given to the poor: his righteousness endures forever'" (latter quote by Paul from Psalm 112:9). Note that Paul says that giving isn't to be done reluctantly or under compulsion (such as when the state imposes taxes for government-run programs for the poor). Another good biblical example of cheerful giving is found in 1 Chronicles 29. In this chapter, King David dedicated much of his wealth to the building of the temple, to be undertaken by his successor, Solomon. He then asked the leaders of the people to ask the people to join him in giving. The response by the people of Israel was breathtaking. We are told in 1 Chronicles 29:9 "Then the people rejoiced because they had given willfully, for with a whole heart they had offered freely to the LORD. David the king also rejoiced greatly."

It can be inferred that God is also pleased by corporate giving through the church or other faith-based organizations. Indeed, Paul encouraged churches in Corinth, Macedonia, and Achaia to take collections for those who were struggling in Jerusalem. Key is whether the giving is done voluntarily and cheerfully. Enthusiastic and cheerful giving was exemplified by the Jewish people when David asked them to give for the building of the temple.

The challenge faced by those with wealth. We have mentioned that the encounter of Jesus with a rich young man (ruler) in Matthew 19 is often cited as an example of how those with wealth are obligated to dispose of that wealth—and give the proceeds to the poor. The young man asks Jesus what he must do to have eternal life. Jesus mentions that he needs to follow the fifth through the ninth commandments, as well as love his neighbor as himself. The young man replied that he had done all these things. Then Jesus told the young man to sell all of his possessions, give the proceeds to the poor, and follow Jesus. This might be seen as Jesus using this incident to teach us that wealth should be more evenly distributed. However, before jumping to that conclusion, note that Jesus didn't ask the young man about whether he had adhered to the first four commandments, dealing with his relationship with God. A more proper interpretation is that Jesus saw into the young man's heart and could see that young man's wealth stood between him and God. Jesus had great compassion for this man and wanted this obstacle to the young man's salvation removed. This example has a parallel elsewhere where Jesus said that if your eye was causing you to sin (placing something else above obedience to God), then you would be better off by plucking it out (Matthew 18:9).

In Luke's version of the encounter with the rich young man (Luke 18:18-27), Jesus says, "How difficult it is for those who have wealth to enter the kingdom of God. For it is easier for a camel to go through the eye of a needle than for a rich man to enter the kingdom of God." But then he goes on to say, "What is impossible with men is possible with God," alluding to it being God's grace that provides salvation. Elsewhere, in Luke 6: 24, Jesus says, "But woe to you who are rich, for you have received your consolation." This is a warning for the rich who place the treasures of this world above God—their riches will turn out to be hollow and cannot satisfy their most basic need.

Returning to Psalm 112 above, the psalmist is telling us that God's blessings of wealth and riches come to those who fear God and take delight in his commandments—those who have their priorities straight.

In keeping with this interpretation, Jesus told the parable of the rich farmer whose harvests had been so abundant that he didn't have sufficient storage capacity to hold them all (Luke 12:16-21). So, he decided to tear down the old barns and build bigger ones to hold it all, believing at which point he will be financially secure and can eat, drink, and be merry. However, God told him that his soul will be taken up that very night and he wouldn't be able to enjoy any of his vast wealth. In telling this parable, Jesus said, "Take care, and be on guard against all covetousness, for one's life doesn't consist in the abundance of possessions (verse 15)." We're told that the farmer had laid up his treasures for himself and wasn't rich toward God (placing riches ahead of God and not obeying God by sharing them with those in need).

In the Beatitudes, Matthew 6: 19-21, Jesus makes it very clear, "Do not lay up treasures on earth where moth and rust destroy and thieves break in and steal, but lay up treasures in heaven, where neither moth nor rust destroys and where thieves do not break in and steal. For where your treasure is, there your heart will be also." And in verse 24, "No one can serve two masters, for either he will hate the one and love the other, or will be devoted to one and despise the other. You cannot serve God and money."

In various other teachings, Jesus conveys that as a person becomes wealthier, the temptation to trust in one's wealth and want more grows, creating a barrier to a right relationship with God by being dependent on Him and trusting Him. For example, in the parable of the sower (Mark: 4:18-19), Jesus tells of the seed that fell among the thorns and eventually was choked out by the thorns. He explains, "And others are sown among thorns. They are those who hear the word, but the cares of the world and the deceitfulness of riches and the desire for other things enter in and choke the word, and it proves unfruitful."

Another parable involves a rich man who had no regard for a starving beggar—Lazarus—who spent his days at the rich man's gate (Luke 16: 19-31). In death, Lazarus joined Abraham in heaven while the callous rich man was tormented in hell, evidently for his disregard of this man in need. Many other passages in both the Old and New Testament similarly point to the need for those with wealth to share with the less fortunate.

The value of work. The production of goods and services requires labor—work. We tend to look at work as a requirement for having income to cover daily necessities, such as food, clothing, and shelter, as well as to cover desirables, such as entertainment and travel. At issue is whether the economic system being examined requires work in return for being able to acquire those goods and services. Some recently have argued that everyone should have a guaranteed basic (minimum) income, regardless of whether they work. Socialist thinkers have been divided on whether work is required of a person as a *quid pro quo* for being able to partake in the output produced in the economy or whether it's optional.

The Bible has something to say about work. In Genesis 3, God describes the consequences of the fall—women will bear substantial pain in childbirth and hard work will be required to provide food for sustenance. In Psalm 104:23, the psalmist says, "Man goes out to work and to his labor until the evening." This is a statement describing the role of work in the normal rhythm of life.

Moreover, the psalmist in Psalm 128: 2 suggests that work is something of value: "You shall eat the fruit of your labor of your hands; you shall be blessed, and it shall be well with you." Or, in Proverbs 10:4, we are told, "A slack hand causes poverty, but the hand of the diligent makes rich." In 1 Thessalonians 4: 11-12, the apostle Paul says, "But we urge you...to work with your hands, as we instructed you, so that you may walk properly before outsiders and be dependent on no one." These latter two verses tell us that we are to seek to work to be self-supporting.

Indeed, this point is made even more emphatically in 2 Thessalonians 3:7-12, where Paul says, " For you yourselves know how you ought to imitate us, because we were not idle when we were with you nor did we did we eat anyone's bread without paying for it, but with toil and labor we worked night and day, that we might not be a burden to any of you. It was not because we did not have that right, but to give you in ourselves an example to imitate. For even when we were with you, we would give you this command: If anyone is not willing to work, let him not eat. For we hear that some among you walk in idleness, not busy at work, but busybodies. Now such persons we command and encourage in the Lord Jesus Christ to do their work quietly and to earn their own living." Paul seems pretty clear that able-bodied people ought to work to provide for themselves, and those who choose not to work are not entitled to receiving the necessities of life from others. It seems pretty obvious from these remarks that Paul would have been highly critical of any member of the communal group described in Acts 2 who took from the common pool without making a good-faith effort to work and contribute meaningfully to the pool.

Elsewhere in the Bible, we find verses that tell us that we get fulfillment from work. Proverbs 14:23 states, "In all toil there is profit, but mere talk tends only to poverty." This is elaborated on in Ecclesiastes 2:24 which says, "There is nothing better for a person than that he should eat and drink and find enjoyment in his toil." Further, in Ecclesiastes 3:22, it says "So I saw that there is nothing better than a man should rejoice in his work, for that is his lot." This is stated somewhat differently in Ecclesiastes 5:18-20, "Behold, what I have seen to be good and fitting is to eat and drink and find enjoyment in all the toil with which one toils under the sun the few days of his life that God has given him, for this is his lot. Everyone also to whom God has given wealth and possessions and power to enjoy them, and to accept his lot and rejoice in his toil—this is the gift of God. For he will not much remember the days of his life because God keeps him occupied with joy in his heart."

On a related matter, Jesus' parable about the landlord who hired workers for his vineyard (Matthew 20:1-16) has implications for the discretion permitted for employers. In this parable, the owner of the vineyard went out early in the day to hire workers for his vineyard and agreed to pay them a denarius for their labor that day—the going market wage for a day's work. As the day progressed, he hired more workers and offered them the same wage—a denarius for working the remainder of the day. These included even those hired an hour before quitting time. The workers hired earlier in the day grumbled about the employer not being fair because those hired at the end of the day received the same pay for only one-twelfth the time spent laboring in the vineyard. The point of the parable was the employer had the right to pay each worker the same, despite the difference in time spent working in the vineyard. Each worker had voluntarily agreed to compensation of one denarius and they had no reason to complain. The employer had a right to be more generous to those hired later. Of course, the deeper meaning of the parable is that God has the sovereign right to dispense the grace of salvation on those whom He chooses, even though some have willingly lived more depraved lives and have waited to their last breath to accept the gift of salvation.

MARKET PRICES IN RELATION TO UNDERLYING VALUE

The Bible doesn't seem to question the validity of prices determined in the market place, with the possible exception of interest rates. For example, when Mary, sister of Lazarus and Martha, anointed Jesus with expensive nard (John 12), Jesus didn't question the value of the nard, said to be worth the equivalent of a full year's wages. Similarly, in the parable of the pearl of great value (Matthew 13), Jesus made the point that the merchant valued the fine pearl so highly that he was willing to sell everything he had to buy it. That market-determined value isn't questioned. In other words, the Bible seems to find that prices determined in the competitive marketplace are acceptable, even when they're very steep.

The issue of charging interest is a little more complicated. In Exodus 22:25, God says "If you lend money to any of my people with you who is poor, you shall not be like a moneylender to him, and you shall not exact interest from him." Note that this commandment is about not charging interest from other Israelites who are poor. Later, Nehemiah condemns Israelites who had charged interest from other Israelites beset by hardships, such as famine (Nehemiah 5). They had their fellow Israelites over a barrel and were exacting what they could—what the market would bear in these circumstances. They were to cease taking advantage of their vulnerable brothers and sisters and were not to charge them interest. Elsewhere, the Bible appears to be okay with the practice of charging market interest rates on loans, especially to non-Israelites. It's important to be clear on this because, as we'll see in Chapter 3, interest rates are prices that play a key role in allocating financial resources to their most valued uses in a market economy.

SUMMING UP

The discussion in this chapter leads to the following conclusions regarding the Bible's treatment of key components of economic systems:

- The pillars of economic systems can be distilled into four categories based on answers to four questions: who owns property, individuals (private property) or the collective (the state); who decides what gets produced with the resources available (individuals and businesses interactively or the state); who decides how goods and services get produced (businesses or the state); and how does production of the economy get distributed (market forces or the state)? In market-based systems, these decisions are largely made by individuals and businesses. In socialist and communist systems, they're made by the state. Fascist systems most closely resemble socialist and communist systems by being centrally directed, but they do allow private ownership of property with limits on its use.

- Today, market-based systems have been morphing in various degrees into welfare states. Welfare states provide safety nets that provide protection against some catastrophic losses and a floor on incomes (redistributing from rich to poor).

- The Bible implies that individuals are endowed with the capacity to make important decisions, including economic decisions (and self-governance choices in democratic political systems). These involve what gets produced and how it gets produced.

- The Bible, in general, doesn't endorse collective ownership of property. It condones private ownership and calls on us to respect the property rights of lawful owners.

- Differences in wealth among individuals have been deemed acceptable in the Bible. Indeed, the Bible gives accounts of certain individuals being blessed by God with vast amounts of wealth.

- However, ownership of wealth isn't to stand between the individual and God—that is, one's wealth shouldn't take precedence over God. Similarly, other things are not to take on more importance in one's life than God, including power, popularity, seeking adulation, beauty, sex, or anything else.

- Wealth and possessions can become distractions that divert people from God. They can keep a person from having a life-giving relationship with our Creator.

- In seeking to please God, all persons—especially those with wealth—are to be generous in caring for those in need. This is to be done willingly and cheerfully. It can be done corporately through a church or other voluntary organization.

- Able-bodied people are expected to work to provide for themselves and not count on others to provide for them. Moreover, work provides a sense of self-fulfillment for the worker, satisfying an inherent God-given desire. Workers, when they voluntarily agree to terms for employment, are to be content with their compensation and not grumble.

QUESTIONS FOR THE DINNER TABLE

1. Should we use the Bible to inform our choice of an economic system?
2. What are your feelings toward capitalism? Socialism?
3. Is inequality a bad thing?
4. Do we want the government to do what God has directed us to do in helping others? Or should we do it ourselves and through our churches?

CHAPTER 2

Market-Based Systems

BACKGROUND

We begin our examination of economic systems by looking at capitalism—market-based systems. This is the system that has characterized the American experience since its earliest days, and the one with which most people have first-hand experience. It's also a system for which there are well-articulated economic principles that describe how the system works in practice and how it stacks up against an ideal. Accordingly, we'll treat a market-based system as a benchmark for evaluating other systems. A more rigorous examination of those economic principles is presented in the appendix.

Interactive system. A market-based system is one in which buyers and sellers interact, be it in the market for goods and services, such as milk or hair styling, or the market for labor, such as auto mechanics or web designers. A market can be highly organized and centralized, as with the New York Stock Exchange, which trades stocks, or it can be fragmented and informal, as with the local market for lawn care.

As noted in the preface, we are using the term "market-based" to characterize this system instead of "capitalist" (a term favored by Karl Marx and Marxists). The latter is a term that tends to stir emotions and conjures up images of workers being subjugated and oppressed by employers in an ongoing struggle between business owners (capitalists who are employers) and workers. However, today, ownership of businesses is widespread. Included among owners are employees, whose ownership takes the form of direct ownership of stock and indirect ownership through pension funds and mutual funds. Also, managers of most large businesses typically have only limited ownership in the enterprise and, in essence, are hired by the shareholders to pursue shareholder interests (some portion of those shareholders are employees of the corporation). And employers know that a satisfied employee is a more productive employee and will be less inclined to bolt for the next available job. In other words, efforts to exploit employees will, in the end, prove to be counterproductive in a competitive labor market.

A market-based system is one in which individuals make choices regarding what they'll purchase and consume. They have a budget based on their income and face prices in the marketplace that must be paid to get the goods and services that they want. Individuals also enter the marketplace when they seek employment. The choice regarding employment determines how much they earn, which, in turn, determines the size of their budget and how much they'll be able to consume.

Individual (private) producers also decide what they'll produce and how they'll produce it. The carrot at the end of the stick for them is earnings—how much profit they can make. Entrepreneurs seek market opportunities that will provide the highest profits. In doing so, they must decide how many workers they'll need, their skill sets, and what they're willing to pay them. Producers also put up some of the funds that are required for the production facilities (capital—plants, machines, software, and research and development) used to make the good or service. For this and the risk they subject themselves to, they expect to be rewarded.

Importance of competition. Key to the functioning of a market system is competition. And key to competition is the ability to enter and exit markets. Profits act as a signal of whether to enter a market. When profits are to be earned, this is a signal that more output is needed.[4] If there are barriers to entry, then shortfalls in production and upward pressure on prices will develop and

---

4   The term "profit" is used here to refer to remuneration for producers of goods and services that exceeds the amount of compensation that they require for the time and effort they put into the business, for the capital that they provide to the business, and for the risks involved. Competition tends to eliminate this excess, as the entry of more producers drives the price down until it converges on the cost of production (keeping in mind that production costs include remuneration to the business owner for the funds they put into the business, for the risks that they shoulder, and for the time and effort that they contribute).

persist. However, when new producers are free to respond by entering that market, supply will expand, and the greater supply will drive the price down to a level commensurate with costs.

Also, this desire to make profits serves as an inducement to innovate—to improve existing products, to introduce new products, and to lower production costs. This plays a key role in improvements to the standard of living of all members of the economy.

Note that a competitive market-based economy doesn't imply that we're playing a zero-sum game. Producers who reap more profits aren't taking them out of the hides of workers. Instead, when they earn more profits, they've added to the overall value of output produced (the size of the pie) and their profit can be viewed as their reward for doing so. The value of extra output that they're responsible for typically exceeds the extra profit they receive, meaning they also have added something that benefits others.

Role of government. There's a common notion that market economies are characterized by laissez-faire in which government sits on the sidelines and has little to do. However, in practice, the government plays a very important role in the success of a market system. It establishes the rules that govern private transactions and provides an adjudication system for dealing with disputes between parties. This entails providing competent and impartial arbiters and enforcement officials. A sound legal infrastructure provides participants in transactions assurances that agreements that they enter into voluntarily will be enforced and that their interests will be protected. This encourages the pursuit of worthwhile economic ventures and is especially important for longer-term arrangements that contribute greatly to growth in living standards.[5] Beyond contributing to a conducive setting for a market economy to operate in, governments have a responsibility to provide those things that won't be provided adequately by the market, such as security of its citizens from domestic and foreign threats. Beyond these, the Bible is very clear about vesting government leaders with the responsibility for establishing justice—ensuring that the rights of all citizens are protected, especially those of widows and the poor. In essence, no one is above the law and the rule of law applies to everyone.[6] An economy for which justice is widely and always practiced has a head start in functioning well.

BIBLICAL BASIS

As noted in Chapter 1, key to differences among economic systems are the following: ownership of property (the means of production)—whether it's privately or collectively owned; who decides what gets produced; who decides how to produce it; and how production is distributed. In a market-based system, all of these are made through the interaction of buyers and sellers in the private sector.

---

5   A growing body of evidence demonstrates that economies with sound legal infrastructures—favorable laws, fair adjudication mechanisms, and stable, supportive political systems—perform appreciably better than others.

6   The notion of the rule of law, which America has long held dear, is very much a biblical principle. The laws that God has given apply to everyone, even kings and other rulers.

From the discussion in Chapter 1, the Bible seems to condone private ownership of property, including assets used in the production process. The Bible also respects the rights of individuals to decide what they want to purchase in the marketplace as consumers, what they choose to do as workers, or what they choose to produce and sell as businesses. It also appears to condone differences in wealth among individuals, so long as it was acquired through legitimate means. Furthermore, Jesus seems to accept that the prices of goods in the marketplace are representative of their value. Thus, the Bible appears to be comfortable with the underpinnings of a market-based system.

THE INVISIBLE HAND

The role of self-interest. Adam Smith was an eighteenth century Scottish moral philosopher, who has come to be regarded as the father of modern-day economics. He published *An Inquiry into the Nature and Causes of the Wealth of Nations* in 1776, which laid the groundwork for our current understanding of how market economies function. In this book, Smith made the statement "It is not from the benevolence of the butcher, the brewer, or the baker that we expect to get our dinner, but from their regard to their own self-interest."

Note that Smith used the term "self-interest," and didn't use the term "greed." He didn't see the pursuit of self-interest to be immoral or tantamount to avarice. Indeed, he saw it as critical to survival. It can be viewed to be similar to the way that we respond to pangs of hunger to ensure that our bodies get essential nourishment or how we respond to pain, which alerts us that something is wrong with our body and requires prompt attention. In other words, self-interest is to greed as satisfying ordinary hunger pangs is to gluttony.

Smith saw human interaction in response to self-interest as producing remarkable outcomes—such as ensuring that our dinner is available each day. He saw this process working as if individual human action was being guided by an "Invisible Hand." Each person, in pursuing self-interest, becomes part of a much broader process that, in the end, leads to social good—indeed, the best social good. This isn't a zero-sum game in which one person's benefit comes at the expense of anyone else. Expressed differently, whenever a person pursues their self-interest, the size of the pie expands and usually by more than that person benefits—meaning that others benefit as well.

The market process coordinates production in a highly decentralized manner, but in a way that results in us getting the food we want at a price that's in line with its cost. Moreover, the pursuit of profit will ensure that costs are held down (resource usage minimized) because lower costs boost the bottom line of sellers.

Specialization and comparative advantage. A factor that serves to lower cost is specialization and the division of labor. The cost, therefore price, of a pair of shoes can be lowered if one worker cuts out soles, another cuts out the uppers, a third dyes the leather, and still another sews the pieces together instead of one person doing all these tasks. That is, more shoes can be produced in a day through such specialization. Furthermore, a good business manager will seek to manage the different skill sets among employees (owing largely to their God-determined diverse talents) by matching those skill sets with the skills required for the different tasks. This, too, leads to an increase in output from the inputs—human resources—available. Economists call this an improvement in productivity.

This is related to the concept of comparative advantage. Some parts of the world have a climate and soil conducive to growing coffee beans (a comparative advantage in growing coffee beans), while other parts of the world have a climate and soil conducive to growing grapes (a comparative advantage in growing grapes). Instead of both regions trying to grow both coffee beans and grapes, there can be more of both goods if the first region focuses on producing coffee and trades some of their coffee output for grapes while the second region focuses on grapes and trades for coffee. The first is a low-cost producer of coffee while the second is a low-cost producer of grapes. This implies that a given amount of resources will be able to produce more coffee and grapes if this type of comparative advantage is exploited—productivity will be enhanced. Another way of viewing this is that consumers' budgets will stretch further— they will enjoy a higher standard of living because their earnings will be higher and the prices of the things they buy will be lower.

Comparative advantage underlies trade among regions and the globalization process. It also underlies trade within a region. Some people have the skills to heal ailing bodies, while others have the skills to wire homes for electricity. Instead of the person with doctor skills doing both healing and electrical work and the person with electrician skills doctoring and doing electrical work, both can achieve a higher standard of living if they focus on what they do best. In essence, the incentive to engage in such specialization will be the ability to earn more by focusing on that line of work for which the person has a comparative advantage.

The Invisible Hand Linked to Impartial Spectator. As noted, Smith regarded himself as a moral philosopher and he regularly taught courses that included the following topics: natural theology, ethics, and jurisprudence. A number of years before he published *The Wealth of Nations,* Smith published *The Theory of Moral Sentiments.* In it, he introduced the concept of the "Impartial Spectator," who works to ensure harmony in the social order as individuals live out their daily lives. In living out their daily lives, they're motivated both by charity toward others and by their own self-interest. Smith believed in the teachings of Jesus, especially His commandment to love our neighbor as our self (Matthew 22: 38).[7] For Smith, this meant not only that we need to have concern for the wellbeing of others, but also that Jesus was saying that it's okay to pursue our self-interest—in loving ourselves. In *The Theory of Moral Sentiments,* Smith says: "The administration of the great system of the universe, however, the care of universal happiness of all rational and sensible beings, is the business of God and not of man. To man is allotted a much humbler department, but one much more suitable to the weakness of his powers, and to the narrowness of his comprehension: the care of his own happiness, of that of his family, his country."

Thus, humans are endowed with reason to be used in caring for themselves, their families, and others. In this pursuit, they seek a system of justice regarding interaction with other persons that protects their interests and is fair to all. As they do, the Impartial

---

7   Smith practiced what he preached and gave substantial amounts to charity. A posthumous discovery of his personal records reveals considerable generosity toward those less fortunate.

Spectator guides the decisions of the various individuals in the community to agree on sets of rules and behavior that serve the common good.

Smith may have been inspired in developing the concept of the Impartial Spectator and later the Invisible Hand by his understanding of the work of the Holy Spirit who dwells in the heart of the believer. In other words, there was an analogy in the sphere of human interaction: Individual humans pursuing their self-interest would make decisions that would be coordinated and harmonized to a degree that goes beyond the understanding of any of the individuals.

Smith's writings suggest that an amazing order resulting from human interaction exists in the economic sphere, as much as in the natural sphere. It can be compared to the vastness and intricate harmony of the cosmos or the volumes of information stored in DNA or the fine-tuned chemical balance that underlies and sustains life. It's highly plausible to conclude that all of these are not accidental outcomes but the work of an intelligent designer (namely God).

It's worth noting that a market-based outcome is characterized as one of consumer sovereignty. Ultimately, what gets produced are those goods and services that consumers want and in the amounts they want, taking into consideration the true underlying costs of producing them. Moreover, the pursuit of better products and lower costs induces further usage of specialization and division of labor and comparative advantage, further enhancing consumer well-being.

Also, the process is comparable to the outcome in a political democracy in which individual voters are sovereign and determine collectively how they are to be governed and who is chosen to govern. Both notions—individual freedom in the marketplace and consent of the governed through the ballot box—can be traced to the Enlightenment. Enlightenment thinkers (of which Smith was one) believed in an underlying natural law that views all persons as being inherently of value and equal in value. Natural law also viewed all persons as being entitled to be free. Enlightenment thinkers had considerable respect for the capacity of all individuals to reason and make sound decisions for themselves. This respect can be traced back to the contributions of Martin Luther, who believed that each person was capable of reading, and with the help of the Holy Spirit, understanding God's word—the Bible.

CURRENT UNDERSTANDING

These days, our understanding of how a market-based system works isn't very different from that articulated by Adam Smith, although the contributions of the past two and a half centuries have helped to fill in a lot of gaps and to more clearly identify linkages. We also have come to better recognize that under some circumstances, free markets don't deliver optimal results.

Competitive markets and efficiency. Based on efficiency principles accepted by economists and described in the appendix, the outcome in a competitive market will be the most efficient one. Without going into great detail, one can summarize the competitive market outcome as one in which consumers will value the last unit of the good or service that they consume at an amount that just matches the cost of producing that item—the sacrifice of other goods and services as a consequence of using resources to produce this last unit. For quantities consumed below this point, consumer valuation of an extra unit will exceed cost; for quantities beyond this point, consumer valuation of the last unit will fall short of cost. At the market outcome, producers will receive compensation for their efforts that represents the market value of their time, a competitive return on the funds (capital) that they have put into their business, and compensation for the risks that they face.

The essential role of prices. What ensures this outcome is that both consumers and producers are responding to price signals. When people want more of a product and there's greater demand for that product, producers will be induced to move more resources into this sector by the higher price that emerges. This results in higher profits, which serve as the inducement for more producers and production. As production expands, the price of the item will retrace its increase and move back into alignment with costs as excess profits disappear. Conversely, if people want less of a product, its price will fall, leading to a decline in profit and a cutback of production. Resources will leave this sector for other sectors of the economy where they can produce things that are valued more highly.

The role of price signals can be seen in the making of a simple BIC ballpoint pen. The pen contains plastic produced in the Netherlands, tungsten from Bolivia, brass from Chile and Australia, and ink compounds from other places. This doesn't include the fuel used in transporting the inputs used in the production process and to distribution points—coal, natural gas, and petroleum from many other parts of the world.

Clearly, many businesses and individuals from all around the globe were involved in producing a single pen. Prices served to coordinate their efforts. If people wanted more pens, the mobilization of resources to produce them would be initiated by the pen manufacturer ordering more of these inputs, putting upward pressure on their prices. This would be a signal for production to be ramped up and expanded for these components or for the inputs to be diverted from other, now less valuable, uses. Underlying this decentralized process is a high degree of coordination, but not one that's fully understood by any of the individual participants. They're simply responding to the prices for the inputs that they confront and are making decisions based on their self-interest. Thus, a competitive market system entails a considerable amount of order, despite the appearance of fragmentation and disarray.

Note further that all the information bearing on the production of this pen that's extant around the globe at any moment is being drawn into the production of this item. For example, if there were a new discovery of tungsten, say, in Indonesia, that's especially well-suited for the production of pens, it would be in the self-interest of the discoverer to sell tungsten to producers of pens, where the price likely will be most favorable. The producer of the pen doesn't have to know about this discovery before the new tungsten source worked its way into the production of pens. What's more, the greater availability of tungsten, after this discovery in Indonesia, would put downward pressure on the price of tungsten, which would induce more demand for and utilization of tungsten. No central planner is needed to achieve this outcome. Indeed, no system involving central planning could incorporate this information in as complete and timely manner as a market system.[8] Moreover, instead of a small army of central planners needing to work on coordinating all these participants, these people can devote their efforts to doing something else—creating value and expanding the pie.

Another example of the working of the price mechanism in a market economy can be seen in how the system promptly responds to an unavoidable disruption to supply—a so-called supply shock. Such a disruption occurred in late-summer 2017 as a result of Hurricane Harvey. The hurricane hit critical parts of Texas and Louisiana, shutting down petroleum extraction in the Gulf of Mexico and refineries in Houston and surrounding cities. In total, about 20 percent of U.S. refining capacity was taken offline by the storm. This meant that millions of businesses and households in that region, dependent on fuel from those refineries, could have been at risk of being without fuel and would have faced serious—perhaps even life-threatening— hardships. But without any central direction, fuel from other regions was diverted to the affected area. This took place because developing shortages in the affected area put upward pressure on fuel prices in that area, which induced suppliers from other parts of the country to redirect supplies in pursuit of these higher prices. As they redirected supplies, prices in other parts of the country

---

8   Fredrich von Hayek, an Austrian Nobel prize winner in economics, illustrated in 1945 the ways in which widely dispersed information is incorporated into decision making throughout a market-based economy. He noted that even information that cannot be articulated easily gets captured into the workings of a market economy. See Hayek, "The Use of Knowledge in Society," *American Economic Review,* vol. 35 (September), pp. 519-30.

were under upward pressure, leading consumers in other parts of the country to voluntarily cut back on consumption. In essence, the interaction of a multitude of businesses and consumers pursuing their self-interest and responding to price movements led consumers around the country to be willing to give up some of their consumption of fuel in order for those in the affected area to also have some. Hardly any of the millions involved had any idea of how this process was working, but their actions were being coordinated by the price mechanism. The coordination of this response was done promptly in a highly decentralized— yet orderly—manner and didn't require the efforts of a single central planner.

Moreover, the role of the price mechanism in coordinating production becomes progressively more important as the complexity of products and their components grows. Increasing complexity is a natural feature of advancing economies. In contrast, this is a mounting challenge to centrally directed (socialist) economies and a huge headwind limiting their development. Information about consumers and their valuation of products, the availability of various types of workers, and the availability of better production processes is widely dispersed, but through the workings of the decentralized market process gets drawn into and utilized in the market outcome. It's extremely hard for a central planner to be aware of all of these pieces of this puzzle and to keep up with the inevitable changes that frequently occur up and down the production process.

Interestingly, professional economists today tend to have a limited appreciation for how the system as a whole operates. The field of economics, like the natural sciences, has become highly specialized and researchers have developed considerable expertise in their respective niches. However, interconnections among all the niches and how the system as a whole functions through the workings of the Invisible Hand is less well understood and appreciated.

Common criticisms. Some find aspects of the price system to be bothersome. The complaint often is that those willing to pay the most are the ones who get the item being sought. Let's look at this carefully. Consider a Christian musical entertainer whose popularity has skyrocketed as she and her music have become better known. As a consequence, the demand for her to put on concerts has grown well beyond the time she has available.

How should she decide which invitations to accept? If she doesn't raise her fee, the number of requests will far exceed the number of concerts she can perform. She will need some other method for deciding which ones to accept. If she does use some other method, such as accepting invitations drawn from a hat or utilizes the first come-first served method, it's likely that some of those she accepts will be for relatively small numbers of attendees or from venues that will be attended by lukewarm concertgoers.

By raising her fee per concert to a level that will bring demand into alignment with the number of concerts she is willing to perform, she can be better assured that more people will be able attend and that those who attend will be more enthusiastic about the opportunity. To some, this may be seen as a Christian entertainer charging what the market will bear or price gouging, but, in practice, it's a way of ensuring a sensible allocation of her precious time and effort. If she's uncomfortable with the extra earnings that she's making, she can donate them to a worthy charity.

Critics of market systems also point out that such systems are characterized by cutthroat competition, implying that members of a market economy are highly vulnerable to losing their means of support—workers can abruptly be thrown onto the streets and businesses can go belly-up overnight.

In the labor market, those allegations are overblown. Jobs are available and people find work. In normal times, 95 percent or more of the labor force is employed and many of those not working are transitioning from one job to another. Job turnover in a dynamic market economy is high. In the United States, more than 60 million people get hired into new jobs each year out of a labor force of approximately 160 million (nearly 40 percent). In bad times, though, those with jobs can drop to 93 percent—or even to 90 percent—and anxiety about holding one's job grows among them. Moreover, some of those with jobs may be working part-time or not holding the kind of job they want. However, even in bad times, employment is available for the bulk of people seeking employment, but they may not be earning as much as they require for maintaining their standard of living.[9]

Turning to businesses, those involved in new businesses are certainly engaged in risky activities, especially those seeking to be highly innovative. The failure rate for such businesses is high, but those who succeed usually do pretty well—well enough for large numbers of prospective entrepreneurs to want to give it a shot. Moreover, failure in one endeavor usually doesn't mean

---

9   For those having difficulty finding work, safety nets have been established in the United States and other market-based economies. The social safety net includes unemployment insurance and programs such as food stamps (Supplemental Nutrition Assistance Program or SNAP).

that subsequent efforts will end the same way. God uses setbacks to help mold us into the person He wants us to be.

Critics have also mentioned that businesses that use Christian business practices won't be able to survive in a market economy characterized by cutthroat competition. Rivals will undersell them with shoddier products having lower costs, they'll misrepresent the quality of those products, and they'll further lower costs by keeping their labor costs down by shortchanging their employees. Christian businesspeople, in contrast, won't be willing to compromise on the quality of their products or how they promote them and will want to be more generous and fair to their employees.

However, experience tells us that, if you cut corners on quality and misrepresent quality, the word will get out and future sales will be impaired. Moreover, when repeat sales are at stake, customers who feel cheated won't return to unscrupulous sellers. On the labor side, we know that contented workers are more productive and less inclined to leave. Thus, employers who show more care for their employees and compensate them better usually find such practices to be good for the bottom line.[10]

Another common criticism is that market economies permit products, such as financial derivatives, that are nothing more

---

10   While a market system will deal with unscrupulous practices by businesses by weeding them out over time, it is also evident that God-fearing participants will choose to engage in ethical business practices. The more such participants, the smoother a market economy will function. Interestingly, management studies are confirming that businesses that show gratitude toward their customers and employees are more successful. Their employees are more productive, loyal, creative, and are absent from the job less often.

than gambling casinos that serve no useful role and cause price volatility. Among such products are futures and options. Actually, these items are risk-shifting devices that enable those unwilling to take on risk to transfer that risk to those more willing and better able to manage the risk. For example, a wheat farmer can protect against a big price drop at harvest—and a potential big hit to their income that year—by locking in a price in the futures market or by acquiring a put option that enables the farmer to sell at a predetermined price at the farmer's discretion. This transfers the risk of a big price drop to another party—the seller of the futures contract or writer of the option. Contrary to popular thinking, the use of derivatives usually stabilizes price movements rather than causes volatility.

Still another criticism involves the environment. It's argued that market economies have been poor stewards of God's creation and are plagued by severe environmental degradation. Disregarding the impact of one's actions on the environment is seen to be good for the bottom line in a capitalist economy. Thus, it's concluded that capitalist systems will be major contributors to environmental degradation. However, the incentives to ignore environmental costs have been recognized for some time, and public policy in market-based systems has been quite effective in altering the incentive structures so that businesses better align their actions with the public interest. Indeed, Western market-based economies overall have among the best environmental ratings in the world today.[11] Near the bottom of the list are

---

11 See 2018 Environmental Performance Index, Yale Center for Environmental Law & Policy (Yale University) and Center for International Earth Science Information Network (Columbia University).

current and former communist and socialist nations. Decision-makers in these nonmarket systems have had similar incentives to ignore the environment, and public policymakers in these nations have been inclined to look the other way.

CORPORATIONS

Corporations in the United States produce around three-fourths of total business output and, thus, play a dominant role in the U.S. economy. There's a common view that corporations are distinct from individuals. However, individuals own corporations. Moreover, as noted in the Preface, this ownership has become widely dispersed among individuals over recent decades, especially as more workers have pension plans and as households have placed more of their savings in mutual funds that hold stock in corporations. More than half of all households own corporate stock, either directly or indirectly—such as through pension and mutual funds.

Owners of shares in corporations are entitled to elect a board of directors to act on their behalf, which is to maximize the value of their shares (which results from maximizing profits). The board of the corporation hires managers to run the corporation and oversees the operations on behalf of the shareholders. In a competitive market system, when managers are seeking to maximize share value, they're guiding resources under their control to the most highly valued uses—those that result in the most output from those resources.

There also is a common view that, if you favor a market-based economic system, you'll naturally be pro-business (especially pro-large corporations) and will favor policies that favor businesses.

Policies that provide for a level playing field and competition for businesses lead to better outcomes for individuals as consumers and workers. However, business leaders often seek policies that favor their businesses at the expense of others and lessen competition. Such policies work against the favorable outcomes of a market economy and lead to suboptimal results. Thus, policies that are favorable to the performance of a market system are going to be policies that promote competition and don't tip the scales one way or another—whether those policies are seen as pro-business or not.

INNOVATION

Innovation is among the types of change that routinely affect economies, regardless of whether the underlying economic system is a market system or it's collectivist. However, market-based systems have greatly outperformed other systems in terms of the innovation that they spawn. There are potentially huge rewards for coming up with new or better products or lower-cost production methods. This has been especially true of the tech sector where a couple of decades ago there were no smart phones, tablets, or social media, and the Internet was just developing. Today, pioneers in these areas dominate the lists of the wealthiest people on the planet.

A successful new product inspires others to emulate the product and make it better. This improves choices for consumers and tends to put downward pressure on prices, a welcome development for consumers. They get products they want at prices that are declining.

Moreover, the potential success of a new product encourages entrepreneurs to utilize their God-given creativity in a way that benefits others. Along the way, it provides those entrepreneurs with an internal sense of accomplishment and fulfillment.

Creative destruction. Joseph Schumpeter, one of the more prominent economists of the twentieth century, referred to this process of innovation in which new and better items replace older ones as "creative destruction."[12] He saw this as an inherent feature of market-based economies. However, he also recognized that this process disrupts the status quo and results in losers—those businesses and workers getting displaced. In economic value terms, the process of innovation expands the size of the pie and, thus, the benefits to those who gain (consumers and innovators) exceed the losses to those who are left behind. Nonetheless, some are worse off as a result of innovation.

A current example can be found in the advertising industry in response to the growing popularity of social media. Those advertising firms that continue to concentrate on television and print media are losing customers to other firms—some relatively new—that can more effectively utilize social media. Employees in the older and more inflexible firms—including newspapers and magazines—are losing jobs and investors are losing wealth.

The United States is leading innovation in the global economy, which is occurring at a blistering pace. Much of this innovation is happening in the information technology and biotech sectors. This, along with globalization, is affecting the

---

12   Joseph A. Schumpeter, *Capitalism, Socialism and Democracy,* (New York: Harper and Row, 1950), pp. 81-86.

distribution of income, benefitting those with technical skills who can create or utilize new technologies.

Automation. Moreover, concerns have intensified about whether rapid innovation in the field of robotics and artificial intelligence (AI) will be displacing large numbers of workers.[13] Robotization and AI processes are working their way up the skill "food chain," displacing people with higher and higher levels of skills along the way. This process will continue and may intensify in the years ahead. In contrast, jobs are being created for those with the skills to automate tasks and for those who operate the new technology. Thus, some are gaining while others are losing. It's worth noting that policies that artificially raise the wages of workers holding lower skill jobs—such as raising the minimum wage—will only add to the incentives for employers to look for ways to automate their jobs away.

Market discipline. During times of rapid change in the economy, an important way in which discipline is placed on producers to respond in a market system is through the financial system. There are several ways in which the financial system disciplines business managers to make needed change and use resources

---

13   It is worth noting that this process of technology displacing workers has been going on for a very long time. Mechanization on assembly lines, in construction, and in agriculture have resulted in many fewer workers doing tasks over many decades. For example, a single farmer today using specialized machines can farm the same parcel of land that required numerous workers a century or so ago—and the yield is many multiples of what it was back then. By and large, this transformation has gone fairly smoothly.

under their control more effectively. In the first instance, the share price of the corporation will fall—especially in relation to its peers— should it be slow at adapting. This will serve as a wake-up call to the managers or to the board of directors of that company, who are charged with representing the interests of the shareholders. Also, if it continues to slip behind, outsiders will see the potential for gain by purchasing enough ownership in the firm to be able to use their leverage to make changes (among them are professional activist shareholders) or to purchase all the shares in the company and take full control. The latter can take the form of an acquisition by another company—perhaps a rival—or by a private equity fund that specializes in corporate turnarounds. Also applying discipline are lenders, such as commercial banks. A business that's falling behind will find it more difficult to get credit, and, when it does, the terms will be stiffer. Taking action to get the business back on track will be the route to getting more favorable treatment from lenders.

Role of self-interest. In all these cases, self-interest serves as the motivator to proceed to make the necessary changes. The advertising industry, mentioned above, is experiencing the intense pressure of survival to make necessary adaptations currently. Obviously, this role of the financial system as a disciplining force becomes more important the more rapid and deep-seated is the change that the economy is undergoing. We see this occurring daily through fast-moving technological advances and globalization. Economic systems that don't rely on the pursuit of self-interest are much more inert in responding to change.

Because progress has its casualties, some would like to see policies implemented that impede change—freeze the system as it is or turn back the clock. However, if successful, that would mean that innovations that are saving lives and enabling us to get more out of life would be casualties.

MARKET IMPERFECTIONS

There are conditions under which a market-based economic system will fall short of the ideal.

Monopoly. One of these is *monopoly*—a single seller in a market. In this case, the monopolist has market power and can restrain sales of output to get a higher price. Consumers pay a higher price and buy less than would be optimal—they value additional amounts of that good or service more that it costs to produce them.

Historically, monopolies have often resulted from government actions that favor the monopolist and restrict entry by other producers. However, it can also come about because the market will only support a single seller—a so-called natural monopoly. The latter occurs when there are very high costs of getting started, but per unit costs fall steadily as production expands. In these circumstances, the firm that's most aggressive in expanding production will be able to sell at lower prices than the competition and, in this way, drive competitors out. Once they're gone, the monopolist will be able to exploit the situation and cut back on production to boost prices.

Public policy in market economies addresses natural monopolies by either regulating a single private supplier or by producing the good or service through a government-owned monopoly. Common examples are utilities such as electricity generation and distribution, water treatment and distribution, and cable TV. Public authorities attempt to ensure that prices to users are comparable to those resulting from a competitive market—commensurate with per unit costs.

Similar outcomes occur if there are only a few sellers—an *oligopoly*. This situation provides incentives for collusion among sellers to collectively restrict supply to be able to get a higher price. Agreements among sellers to restrict supply are called cartels. While there are powerful incentives for sellers to collude, there also are powerful incentives to cheat in order to sell more and get more profits. This undermines the cartel. The Organization of Petroleum Exporting Countries (OPEC) is a cartel among governments of major global oil producers and it has had a longstanding problem of cheating among its members—producing more than their assigned quota in order to get additional revenue at the expense of other members of the cartel. Within nations, public policy in the form of antitrust policy seeks to curtail the ability of sellers to collude to achieve higher prices. Antitrust policy also addresses attempts to monopolize industries.

Public goods. A second form of imperfection occurs for so-called *public goods*. A public good is one for which, once produced, it becomes available to other users at no extra cost. Unlike ordinary goods and services that are said to be rival—that is, if one person gets an orange from a street vendor, it's not available to others—public goods are non-rival. Radio broadcasts satisfy these criteria. Once a radio signal has been sent out for one person, it's available to others at no additional cost to the broadcaster.

National defense satisfies this criterion. Once a national defense system is in place, additional people can be protected at no extra cost. A public good situation gives rise to the so-called free-rider problem; any beneficiary of this service will receive it whether they contribute to its cost or not. This leads to difficulty in being able to collect enough from consumers to cover costs, which results in a suboptimal amount of the public good.

As a consequence, there's a role for government to become involved. Governments routinely provide for national defense. But, in the case of radio, private radio stations have long been able to survive in market economies, based on advertising revenue. This suggests that being a public good isn't a sufficient reason for government to be the provider.

Externalities. A third form of imperfection, touched on above, occurs when there are so-called *externalities*. An externality occurs when the production or consumption of an item affects third parties—those other than the seller or the buyer. A common example is pollution in the production of a product that affects the quality of air or water used by others. That is, third parties are adversely affected by the production of this item, but the producer of the product doesn't take the interests of third parties into consideration. To deal with these situations, public policies are established, such as placing taxes on production, that, in effect, "internalize" the externalities or by restricting the amount of effluents that a producer can discharge.

The presence of externalities isn't a sufficient reason for public policy to intervene. A Nobel-prize economist, Ronald Coase, argued that the parties involved when externalities are present might voluntarily agree to deal with the problem in a way that no one ends up being worse off.[14] An example of such a voluntary solution occurs regularly in homeowners' associations (HOAs). Members of communities with homeowners' associations voluntarily agree to take certain actions—such as keeping up their yard—or refraining from certain actions—such as painting the exterior of their homes with garish colors—in return for being assured that their neighbors are subject to these same conditions. The way members of the community take care of their property affects others in the community—an externality—and this has been an effective way in which everyone in the community can be better off (the enjoyment received by the more attractive community under the HOA exceeds the disadvantages of the restrictions and fines homeowners voluntarily accept).

Business cycles and financial crises. A fourth type of problem faced by market-based economies is *business cycles and financial crises.* Business cycles are ups and downs in the broader economy that give rise to swings in employment, incomes, and wealth. Some of these downturns in the broader economy are precipitated by financial crises in which there are large financial losses and sharp cutbacks in lending by banks. Prior to 2008, many analysts had come to the view that business downturns and financial crises had been tamed, but the financial crisis and Great Recession of 2008 and 2009 demonstrated that this pronouncement was premature. Numerous reforms were made in the wake of this episode, and these may have reduced the scope for a recurrence.

---

14   Ronald Coase, "The Problem of Social Cost," *Journal of Law and Economics,* 1960, vol. 3, issue 1. Pages 1-44.

Inequality. A fifth shortcoming of a market-based economy that's frequently mentioned is *inequality of income and wealth.* Inequality was discussed in Chapter 1 and is touched on below.

One can summarize this section by noting that market-based economies contain some blemishes—not too surprising in a fallen world. However, God has provided people with cognitive skills to address these imperfections through public policy measures. Worth keeping in mind is that instances in which market shortcomings exist don't always call for a public policy response. Often, the cure can be worse than the disease, and, in some cases, the private sector will address the problem by itself.

INCOME AND WEALTH DISTRIBUTION

As noted in Chapter 1, market-based systems result in marked differences in income and wealth, more so for wealth.[15] When it comes to labor earnings, people get paid in keeping with their productivity—the value of what they contribute in the production process. Much of the differences across people can be explained by:

---

15   The terms income and wealth are often used interchangeably, but income is distinct from wealth. To illustrate, suppose that you have a $100 savings account that pays you 2% interest. The $2 that you earn each year on this account is a contribution to your income, while the $100 balance in your account is a component of your wealth. The distribution of wealth is less equal than the distribution of income, importantly because people accumulate assets by saving over their working lives. In other words, people who are older will tend to be wealthier, implying that changes in the age distribution of the population will result in changes in the distribution of wealth even if incomes were the same across individuals.

- Age. More experienced and mature people are more productive and have accumulated greater savings, which generates more income for them.

- Industriousness. Some people worker longer and harder than others. This can be a big factor in one's overall productivity.

- Education and nurture. Some people are more productive because they have acquired more formal education, footing education costs and sacrificing earnings while attending school. Also, many have gotten more help in formal learning and in acquiring habits and skills that are valued in the marketplace from parents or relatives. Attitudes toward work also are important and can be nurtured by family members.

- On-the-job training. Such training is more practical—hands on—than formal education, but importantly contributes to one's productivity. Some occupations, such as construction trades, have well-structured apprenticeship programs that involve training on the job.

- Health. Healthy workers are more productive, work more hours, and do better than unhealthy ones. In some cases, they're healthier because they've taken better care of themselves. In others, they've been endowed with healthier genes.

- Risk. Some jobs entail more risk than others and workers in those occupations get compensated for the risk. Police and firefighting are examples of physical risk. Entrepreneurs are examples of financial risk.

- Appeal of the work. Some jobs are perceived to be very pleasant and others much less so. Musicians, who love to perform, often are willing to do so for meager compensation, while over-the-road truckers require greater compensation to compensate for being away from home and family and for the long hours and tediousness of the job.
- Physical and mental ability. Some have been blessed with more than others. A gifted professional athlete can earn a fortune in only a season.
- Inheritance. Some have inherited more wealth than others.

A major issue to be resolved is whether differences in income and wealth resulting from these factors are acceptable. If so, the resulting inequality associated with a market-based economy isn't to be regarded as a shortcoming. However, there are other factors that can lead to inequality—such as racial or ethnic discrimination—that are not tolerable.[16]

Some statistics on income distribution can be highly disturbing. For example, the income of the bottom one-fifth of the population is less than 5 percent of the total for all Americans

---

16 Historically, government policies have often enforced racial and ethnic discrimination and competition has led to those being discriminated against being provided opportunities. A good illustration of the role of competition is Jackie Robinson breaking the color barrier in major league baseball. The Dodger organization wanted to field a more competitive team and realized that adding Jackie to the roster would do just that. For more on this issue, see Thomas Sowell, **Basic Economics,** Basic Books (New York, 2015), pp. 209-215.

while the top one-fifth receives more than half. It needs to be noted that this represents a snapshot as of a point in time and that some of the people at the top end and the bottom end in one period appear elsewhere in the income distribution in other periods. Also, a large segment of those at or near the top are older and, earlier in their lives, were in lower ranges. In other words, only a portion of those at the lower rungs, at any one point in time, are stuck there throughout their lives.

Public policy in market economies has sought to bring about more equality through tax systems that tax people with higher incomes more heavily and by providing various types of assistance to those with lower incomes.[17] Economies that have gone down this path have been labeled welfare states—the subject of Chapter 5.

It should be noted that differences in income are not confined to market economies. All types of economic systems experience sizable differences in income, though, in many cases, those differences get masked.

---

17 The Congressional Budget Office estimates that federal tax and transfer (income support) policies have had a significant impact on distribution. This has been done through programs that raise the means of low-income persons appreciably and reduce the means of higher-income groups by a sizable amount. The raw data on income distribution show inequality becoming greater over time in the United States. However, when public tax and transfer programs are included, there's not much of a discernible trend. More on this in Chapter 5.

WORK

In a market-based economy, people get rewarded for work. And the need to earn enough to provide for one's well-being is a powerful motive for individuals to seek work. As noted in Chapter 1, the Bible looks favorably on work. Indeed, Paul, in 2 Thessalonians 3, is pretty clear in saying that able-bodied people should work if they want to eat.

As noted, in a market economy, the amount that workers get paid will depend on their productivity. An individual's productivity, in turn, depends on experience, education and training, health, and whether that person's fundamental abilities are aligned with the requirements of the job. Also, other factors, such as risk and the degree of unpleasantness of the work, will increase earnings.

But the amount of earnings isn't the deciding factor for choosing an occupation for many individuals. They may feel a sense of calling to a certain field or have a passion for doing a certain job and are willing to accept lower pay to be able to work in that field. In a market system, individuals are free to make such choices and are not compelled to work elsewhere because someone else believes they can contribute more somewhere else.

An issue that comes up in the context of a market economy is whether workers need to act collectively to avoid abuses by employers—do they need trade unions? It has been argued that employers have leverage over employees and use this to hold down their pay, work them excessive hours, and perhaps subject them to safety and environmental hazards. The argument has been that, if the employees are able to bargain collectively, they can level the playing field and their interests can be more effectively protected. For these reasons, public policy in market economies has protected the right of workers to unionize.

Unions have raised compensation for their members. However, this has made union labor more expensive to employers, and employers in the unionized sectors have responded by hiring fewer workers. This has meant that workers not able to find employment in the unionized sector must seek work elsewhere, where they put downward pressure on wages in those sectors as they compete with other workers for jobs available. This tends to create differences in the distribution of income.

In a competitive labor market, workers who believe that they're being treated unfairly by their employer are free to leave that employer and go elsewhere. The prospect of losing good employees and the need to find replacements—at significant cost—acts as a check on employers that's not present in other economic systems.[18]

Interestingly, unionization in the private sector has been on the decline for decades. Currently, only around 6 percent of private sector employees are unionized, down from more than one-third in the 1950s. Unionization has been more common in the manufacturing sector, and less so in the service sector of the economy. Younger workers haven't shown much interest in being members of unions and the less-unionized service sector

---

18 Another factor that has reduced employer leverage over employees has been the marked shift in employer-provided pension plans—away from defined benefit (DB) plans and toward defined contribution (DC) plans. Under standard DB plans, employees tend to be locked into their employer because sticking with that employer provides increasingly attractive pension benefits. Not so with DC plans because pension benefits are not similarly backloaded.

has expanded over this time. Also, younger workers are inclined to change jobs more frequently than their parents and, in these circumstances, don't see joining a union to be beneficial over their working life. At the same time, employers have come to realize the benefits of satisfied employees and have used compensation and other measures to attract and retain employees. Unions have been much more successful in organizing government workers, where more than one-third of federal, state, and local employees are members of unions.[19]

SUMMING UP

- Market-based economies rely on incentives that encourage people to pursue their self-interest in ways that lead to high levels of output and economic growth. The average standard of living is high in these economies, although the dispersion around that average can also be high. That dispersion relates significantly to differences in productivity, which, to an important degree, relate to choices that people make. But some differences in productivity also result from conditions outside the control of the individual.

- Prices guide decisions in a market economy. They're determined by the interaction of demand and supply.

---

19 This may be in the process of changing as a result of a 2018 Supreme Court ruling in which the Court declared that public sector employees cannot be compelled to pay union dues. An ongoing concern about public sector unions is that these unions make contributions to the campaigns of the very political officials who make decisions about the compensation that their workers receive through collective bargaining.

They serve to ration the available supply. But they also serve as signals to expand or contract that supply, which guides resources into or out of that sector. It's a very decentralized process, but one that achieves a high level of coordination. Ironically, those involved in the process typically are unaware of how vast the participation of other players and the high degree of coordination are. Self-interest ensures that the information available at any time, regardless of how dispersed it happens to be, is fully utilized in the production process. Adam Smith referred to this coordination as the work of an Invisible Hand.

- The pursuit of self-interest brings about low prices and a high degree of efficiency. Moreover, producers have an incentive to apply their creativity to innovation—new and better products or discovering lower-cost means of production. The material rewards can be substantial, as can be the sense of fulfillment. Such innovation fosters growth, but also results in some being losers—creative destruction.

- Market outcomes are not always optimal. Certain conditions—notably, monopoly, public goods, and externalities—can impede the achievement of efficiency. In these situations, there often is a role for government to shape public policy to correct the problem. People are endowed by their Creator with the cognitive ability to address these shortcomings through public policy.

- All types of economies experience inequality, including market-based economies. Public policy in market economies has aimed at reducing inequality through taxing higher-income people more heavily and transferring these funds through public assistance programs to those who are poorer.

QUESTIONS FOR THE DINNER TABLE

1. How do prices play an essential coordinating role in a market system? How does all available information get worked into a market system? How does this relate to the role of the Invisible Hand?

2. Why is there inequality in a market-based system? Can such inequality be justified, or does it need to be addressed though government policy?

3. What do you think about the "creative destruction" that takes place routinely in a market-based economy? Does it make us better or worse off?

4. Are big businesses a threat? Are they all monopolies? Should they be treated differently than other businesses?

5. How would you characterize the response of private businesses to the Covid-19 pandemic?

CHAPTER 3

Socialist Systems

BACKGROUND

Socialist systems are characterized by collectively owned property and collective decisions regarding what gets produced, how it gets produced, and how it gets distributed to members of the economy. This generally is done by a planning agency; hence, socialist economies are frequently labeled centrally planned economies. The political system of the country determines accountability of the planning agency. In the case of a democracy, the planning agency would be accountable to elected leaders. In other cases, it would be accountable to those who control the state. In a single-party state, it's to the party—the custodian of the ideology—itself.

Proponents of socialist systems have argued that these systems can be at least as efficient as market systems.

It's noteworthy that, while there are well-developed and time-tested theoretical underpinnings of market-based systems, the economic theory underlying socialist systems is, at best, sketchy. The theory that does exist largely piggybacks on that for market systems. The absence of coherent underlying principles for a socialist system can explain why proponents of socialism so often have difficulty defining what a socialist system actually is. It happens to be what's in the eye of the beholder, and that varies widely.

In this chapter, we'll examine the biblical arguments for a socialist system and evaluate the economic arguments for socialism. We'll also touch on the actual experience with socialist systems.

In the next chapter, communism and fascism will be examined. Communism is a form of socialism, and fascist systems also have claimed to have their roots in socialism.

Today, in America, it has become somewhat fashionable to label oneself as a socialist along the lines of Bernie and AOC. However, these self-proclaimed socialists haven't spelled out what they mean by the term. They've been much clearer about wanting to use government to engage in wholesale income redistribution, transferring substantially more from the rich to lower-income persons. They also have been clear about wanting to impose draconian environmental measures. Whether they intend this to be achieved through heavily regulated private producers or through the state taking over the means of production broadly—as in traditional views of socialism—has not been spelled out. One area where they're advocating a state takeover is healthcare, wanting the government to replace private insurers and control health care providers.

BIBLICAL BASIS

Proponents of socialism often refer to the account of the early Christian community in Acts 4, discussed at some length in Chapter 1. The biblical account mentions that the members of this community pooled everything in common. They sold their possessions and people took from the common pool as they had need. Private property was transformed into commonly held (communal) property. This episode has inspired social experiments among Christian groups, such as the Amana colonies in Iowa.[20] It evidently also inspired Karl Marx to claim that in a utopian communist system, "From each according to his ability, to each according to his needs," which seems to be a paraphrase of Acts 4:35. As noted in Chapter 1, the Bible doesn't prescribe common ownership of property but does presume private ownership. Also, the episode in Acts may be interpreted to be a glimpse of what life will be like in the millennial kingdom, once Jesus returns—not something that's sustainable on this side of that kingdom.

The other biblical account that frequently gets mentioned as an endorsement for redistribution policies is the encounter between Jesus and the rich young ruler. In this account, Jesus

---

20   The Amana colonies in Iowa were an outgrowth of a German Christian group that left Germany as a result of persecution. They settled for a time in New York State, before moving to Iowa. The colonies established a constitution that specified the terms under which members would live as a commune. This system lasted nearly a century, until the 1930s. By then, a growing number of community members wanted to strike out on their own—no longer be confined by the restrictions of the communal system—and the communal system was dissolved.

tells the young man to sell all his wealth and give the proceeds to the poor. This could be regarded as an indictment of wealth and an endorsement of a more equal distribution of wealth. However, as mentioned in Chapter 1, Jesus seems to be telling us that we should remove from our lives anything that stands between God and us. In this case, Jesus could see that the obstacle was the man's wealth, as it has been for many others before and since that time. But, elsewhere in the Bible, God blessed various prominent patriarchs with substantial amounts of wealth, as they had their priorities in order.

On balance, it's hard to see how the teachings of the Bible support socialism. But, as also noted in Chapter 1, the Bible is very clear in expressing the importance of caring for the poor and others in need.

ECONOMICS OF SOCIALIST SYSTEMS

Proponents of socialist systems have argued that these systems can replicate the efficiency of market systems. Indeed, some argue that socialist systems may even be able to surpass the efficiency of market-based systems because they don't have to pay out profit.[21] Or incur wasteful marketing expenses.[22]

---

21 The impression conveyed is that profit represents a totally superfluous payment to business owners. However, what gets labeled profit largely is compensation for the time that the owner puts into the business, the risk that the owner confronts, and the funds that the owner has invested. Thus, it isn't superfluous but is payment for actual resources devoted to producing things of value.

22 The role of advertising and marketing in a market economy is somewhat controversial. To some, it represents a pure waste of resources, and just

Some also make the argument that consumers, left to their free will, will select things in the marketplace that are not in their best interest. For example, some people will select potato chips or other junk foods over more healthy vegetables and fruits. Because a socialist system has more control over what consumers have to choose from, it's argued that socialism can better ensure that the goods and services available to the public are wholesome. Moreover, such an omniscient central planner would be able to avoid the marketing costs incurred in a market-based economy because the planner knows what best meet the true needs of individuals and doesn't need to convince people that they should select a particular product over another. Some advocates of socialism also have argued that socialist systems create a better sense of togetherness, as individuals are not competing with one another and are more focused on the common good.

A major issue in a socialist system involves whether such a system can be designed to replicate the coordinating role of prices in a market economy. As noted in the previous chapter, prices play a vital role in a market-based system. They guide resources to their most highly valued uses. If consumers want more pizza and fewer cheese sandwiches, producers of cheese will get more for their output by directing it to pizza makers. For business managers, prices inform decisions about how to undertake production. A producer of electricity can use coal, natural gas, or petroleum as fuel to generate electricity. If,

---

adds to the price of the good. Others note that advertising is a way in which, in a world of scarce information, sellers are able to provide valuable information about their products to potential buyers, enabling buyers to make better choices in the marketplace.

for example, new discoveries of natural gas lower the price of natural gas, producers have an incentive to shift toward natural gas. At issue is whether anything comparable will occur in a socialist system.

In a socialist system, consumers and producers may or may not confront prices, depending on how the system is organized.

Bypassing prices. Under the central planning model that was developed in the Soviet Union and adopted in various other places, prices didn't play much of a role. The central planning agency made the key decisions regarding what and how much of each good to produce. The agency also had responsibility for directing the resources that were made available to plant managers for production of goods and how goods got distributed to people.

How does this agency go about making all those decisions? This is a mind-boggling task. What kinds of specific goods and services should be produced? How much of each item should be produced? How are the resources available to the economy— workers, buildings, machines, land, and materials— going to be allocated among the many producers?

In principle, the central planning agency could replicate the efficient outcome of a market economy if it had all the information available to the various disparate producers and consumers in a market-based economy. This includes the preferences of consumers, the methods available for the production of each item, and the amounts of the various resources that are available for production in the economy. A system of equations linking all of these pieces could be assembled, solved, and an optimization achieved. This would give the central planner the amount of each good or service that should be produced and the amount of each input needed to produce that amount.[23] It would also direct distribution—who would get the items produced.

In practice, however, such equations are simplified approximations of reality, and don't come anywhere close to capturing all the information that's utilized in a decentralized market setting. Moreover, the equations are a snapshot at a point in time. And the things that matter for achieving desirable results—efficient production methods, consumer preferences, and resource availability—are constantly changing. Even with the proper incentives, planners are constantly going to be playing catch up, whereas the participants in market-based systems have it in their self-interest to be on top of and respond to those changing situations.

NOW OR THE FUTURE?

Decisions have to be made in any economy about whether to consume now or in the future. If the decision is to consume more (have a higher standard of living) in the future, consumption today will have to be sacrificed. The resources that are released from producing current consumption

---

23 The solution to such a system of equations would have, as a by-product, a complete set of so-called shadow prices for each item produced and for each of the inputs. Each shadow price would represent the underlying value of a final good or an input. For example, Marx measured value in terms of the amount of labor embodied in the item—the cumulative number of labor hours required for the production of an item— as the value of the item.

goods are now available for producing capital (investment) goods that enable more to be produced (and consumed) in the future. That is, inputs, such as labor and capital, can be used for producing consumption or investment goods.[24]

The decision regarding the production of consumer versus capital goods is key to economic growth and future output. The more capital goods that are produced in the current period, the more output that can be produced in the future—consumer or capital goods—and the higher will be the future standard of living. Thus, there's a trade-off between current consumption and future consumption—the more of one, the less of the other. The planner must make a determination about how much gets allocated to addressing current wants versus providing for a better standard of living in the future.

That decision could be based on trying to gauge the sentiment of consumers regarding their preference for current versus future consumption, or the planning agency may believe that it can make better decisions than individuals themselves. Some have favored having the central planner make the allocation between current and future consumption because they believe that individuals are myopic and don't adequately provide for the future—they save too little. Indeed, the planners in the Soviet Union didn't allow much to be devoted to consumption.

---

24   Intermediate goods are also produced. They represent products that have been made and have yet to be transformed further before they're final consumer or capital goods. For example, a steel mill produces steel—an intermediate good—that is used in the production of automobiles (a consumer good) and machines (a capital good).

They wanted to build an industrial powerhouse by devoting much of current output to production of capital goods. It didn't work out as well in practice because the process was highly inefficient. More on that in the next chapter.

In contrast, in a market economy, the decision regarding current versus future consumption is an individual decision. The cumulative amount of saving by individuals represents the total amount of funds that becomes available to producers for investment in their businesses. This amount gets rationed to producers through a price mechanism—the level of interest rates. Those willing to pay the interest rate are the ones getting the funds to undertake investment. In practice. They'll be the ones having the investments with the highest returns and making the greatest contributions to growth in output. The problem is solved by the interaction of numerous businesses and consumers (savers) through the decentralized marketplace—the financial system.

Utilizing prices. The above discussion looks at a socialist planning system that doesn't rely on prices. One could, however, devise a socialist system that uses prices to guide economic decisions, mimicking the role of prices in a market system.[25] It would be a challenge, though, to construct incentive structures,

---

25 A prominent twentieth century Polish economist, Oskar Lange, developed a scheme for a socialist economy to replicate the results of a competitive market economy using prices as an allocator of final goods and services and labor. O. Lange, **On the Economic Theory of Socialism,** Minneapolis: University of Minnesota Press, 1938.

especially for producers, that would match those in a market economy. This is easier said than done.

In sum, in a socialist system, the Invisible Hand that's at work in a market economy is short-circuited. The socialist system foregoes the coordinating function of markets, that comes about through freely flexible prices, and lacks the ability of a market system to utilize all of the information that's extant and dispersed throughout the economy.

Our discussion above presumes that the objective of a socialist economy is to replicate the efficiency of a market economy. As noted, some have argued that individuals often don't make good decisions for themselves, and it would be better to have others with superior knowledge and wisdom make decisions for them—such as ensuring a healthier diet of foods. It also has been suggested that consumers in a market economy are myopic and don't save enough; this implies that there won't be enough resources set aside for capital formation (which improves economic growth and the standard of living in the future). Furthermore, there may be objectives that are not achieved in a market-based system. Included here might be a closer sense of togetherness, more economic security, lessened intensity of competition, or projecting a higher national profile on the international stage, say, through more dominant national sports teams. Proponents argue that the central planners can factor these objectives into the plan and the result will be a superior outcome.

DISTRIBUTION

Much like other aspects of socialist economic systems, the principles for distribution are not well articulated. As noted in Chapter 1, achieving more equity in distribution may be meant to imply that everyone gets exactly the same amount of everything. This could be done by taking total production of each item and dividing it equally among all members of the economy. Each person could be given ration coupons entitling that person to exchange the coupons for their proportionate share of the total output of each item. Because tastes and needs differ across individuals, there would need to be rules about whether individuals can exchange items they don't want for those things that they want. For example, if someone is a vegetarian and another a hearty meat eater, will they be able to exchange meat for vegetables, and, if so, will there be any restrictions on the terms of such an exchange—that is, will the planning agency require that a certain amount of vegetables exchange for a pound of meat?

Alternatively, people can be permitted to choose among the goods produced by the collectively owned producers. This can be achieved by providing each person with a certain amount of general purchasing power, money, and then let each person shop for the things that they want and pay for the items with money.

A problem here is determining the price for each item that's sold. Will it be based on cost, and, if so, how is cost determined? In a market economy, the cost of inputs—including labor— is determined by the interaction of the supply of and demand for those inputs and is the basis for determining prices. In a competitive setting, the cost of those inputs will reflect their value in alternative uses. Relying on prices in a socialist system runs the risk that the price selected may not balance demand with supply. As a consequence, demand may exceed supply (shortages occur) or demand may fall short of supply (inventories of unsold goods pile up).

A common argument made by proponents of socialism is that things should be free, at least, certain items such as college, health care, and housing. The problem with this idea is that inevitably the amount that will be demanded will exceed the amount produced. When the price of something goes down, the amount people want of that item invariably goes up. When the price falls to zero, demand grows to the saturation point. And more of that item needs to be produced to avoid a shortage. If no price is to be charged for these items, the economy will, under the best of circumstances, lack the resources needed to meet demand. In a market-based economy, the job of prices is to bring demand into alignment with what gets produced.

But if the price is zero, this isn't an option. Some other rationing mechanism must be used. This can take the form of first-come, first-served (queuing).[26] Or it can be done by lottery (leaving the decision of who gets the scarce item to chance)

---

26 In the Soviet Union, consumer goods were rationed through a very cumbersome process. It required individuals to stand in long lines to select the item(s) they wanted, stand in another line to pay a cashier, and then return to the original line to exchange the cashier's receipt for the item. The items had a price, but the price was well below a market-clearing price. This procedure was applied to each category of goods, such as meat, and had to be repeated for other categories, such as dairy products and baked goods.

or by placing the decision in the hands of public officials.[27] Political considerations can also enter in—is the person loyal to those in control? In the Soviet Union, there were national goals of military superiority and Olympic championships and persons who aided in achieving those goals received priority in the allocation process—better apartments, classier cars, and prized vacations.

Another set of issues arises regarding whether some are entitled to more than others. Should physically large persons get more food than those who are small? If so, how much more? Should they get less of other items? If a person works harder, should that person be entitled to more goods and services? What if that person is more gifted and can produce more? What if a person wants to consume more now and is willing to forego consumption in the future? Will this person be permitted to have access to more goods now in return for less later? And if so, what's the tradeoff—how much must be sacrificed in the future for the additional consumption now? These are situations that will result in inequality in consumption, and likely will impinge on personal freedom to make choices, including those involving one's health or life. Who makes these decisions and on what grounds?

27　Leaving the decision of who gets the available items opens up the process to corruption. Those with the authority to make the decisions have an enormous opportunity to personally profit from it. History is filled with this form of rationing, degenerating into widespread corruption. Communist systems have been especially plagued by corruption.

SHORTCOMINGS OF SOCIALISM

In our discussion of socialism above, we've seen that socialist systems lack a set of well-articulated principles for how they are to be organized and for how essential decisions are to be made. Moreover, many of the decisions that need to be made are based on personal values, which differ widely among persons. As a consequence, such a system won't escape strains among its members. Furthermore, the goal of equality will prove to be elusive.

A basic issue with a socialist system is whether the collective—the planning agency—is capable of making better decisions than individual members themselves. Do those in control know more about what's best for individuals than individuals themselves? Also, will central planners and the plant managers they select be able to make better decisions about how to produce items than entrepreneurs pursuing their self-interest? Proponents, though, argue that overarching social objectives don't get adequately considered by individuals in their personal economic decision making and that central planners can take these into consideration—such as measures that enhance national pride. In any event, turning over decisions to a central planner comes at the expense of personal freedom.

Beyond this is the issue of incentives. This applies at all levels of economic decision making. It applies to workers. If all are going to be compensated the same, many will decide to do as little as possible and will attempt to avoid taking risks or doing tasks that are messy and unpleasant. Some argue that such shirking is an unfounded criticism, but a great deal of research on actual human behavior demonstrates that when people get income unrelated to work effort, they cut back on the amount of time spent working. For example, how many times have you heard of a person who wins the lottery and then announces that they're quitting work? They can now enjoy the lifestyle they want whether they work or not, and many choose not to work. This likely was behind Paul's statement that a person who chooses not to work shouldn't be entitled to what has been produced by others.

Incentive problems also apply to managers of production facilities—plant managers. What motivation do they have to adopt methods that reduce the amount of resources used in production (that is, lower costs)? If they were to be motivated by being allowed to share in the gains from making improvements—being allowed to consume more—this would contribute to inequality, which would conflict with the socialist goal of equality. As noted in the previous chapter, being able to adapt to change becomes more important the more rapid change is. And the world today is marked by a breathtaking pace of change. Without adequate incentives, adaptation will be sluggish at best given incentives in a socialist system.

Related to this, incentive problems also arise when it comes to innovation, which stimulates change and plays a key role in spurring improvements in the standard of living of people. Entrepreneurs perform this role in market economies by attempting to translate their creativity involving new and better products into something of value that will pass the market test and yield large profits. There are considerable risks in doing so—in practice, most start-up businesses fail—but the potential payoff is enough for them to willingly incur the risks. Moreover, many find it highly satisfying when they create something that's valued by others, apart from the financial reward.

How can a socialist system internalize incentives for innovation? Will innovators be sufficiently motivated by the sense that they're contributing to the greater good? Or will they need more? If so, can central planners calibrate the benefit from an innovation? Will the reward be related to that calculation or will the planning agency decide on some other basis? Will this be sufficient to induce innovation? Again, rewarding useful innovations will compromise equality objectives because the innovators will be given more.

Beyond these considerations, mistakes are inevitably going to be made in any economy, for, in an imperfect world, humans are prone to making errors. In a market economy, these mistakes will be translated to the bottom line of the business promptly— losses will occur. If the business doesn't respond quickly, the losses will accumulate and lead to failure—bringing this mistake to an abrupt end. In a socialist system, there's more scope for mistakes to be perpetuated because there's no such automatic corrective mechanism. Moreover, there are incentives to cover them over. Depending on the degree of transparency and accountability that that's built into such a system, the corrective mechanism may take an extremely long time to acknowledge and address the problem.

Moreover, the scope for corruption is great when nonmarket methods are used to determine who gets the items that are in short supply. And in a socialist system, there will be a multitude of goods in short supply. The full sweep of history demonstrates that corruption is virtually irrepressible when there are so many opportunities for under-the-table gains. Beyond ordinary corruption, there's considerable scope for using the vast levers of government in a socialist system to reward those who choose to comply with the authorities and punish those who do not. Even in the United States, with its more limited national government and greater transparency, there have been numerous scandals in which political friends have been rewarded and enemies punished.

THE RECORD

As the above discussion suggests, the historical record of socialism has been fraught with disappointment.[28] The poster child for socialist disaster has been Venezuela. To begin with, Venezuela was endowed with massive amounts of oil reserves, among the largest in the world, and, under an earlier market-based economy, had one of the highest standards of living in the world. Venezuela moved to a centrally directed economy in fits and starts over several decades. And, as it did, stagnation set in. In the early years of this century, Hugo Chavez, then president, sharply stepped up the move to socialism and the Chavez agenda was continued under his hand-picked successor, Nicolas Maduro. As central control increased, the economy contracted and shortages of essentials—food and medicine—ballooned, as did crime waves and corruption. Owing to food shortages and illnesses, it's estimated that the average weight of Venezuelans declined eighteen pounds in 2016 and another twenty-four pounds in

---

28 One of the earliest socialist communities was introduced in the early nineteenth century in New Harmony, Indiana by Robert Owen, a Welsh industrialist. Like Marx and Lenin who followed him, Owen believed that people needed to be transformed radically if a socialist system was to flourish. His New Harmony experiment lasted only two years, evidently because members continued to pursue their self-interests. Notably, Owens was opposed to religion, including Christianity, but later became a spiritualist.

2017. The political elite have been spared these deprivations, and, indeed, have been able to spirit billions of dollars into their personal accounts outside the country. Meanwhile inflation has soared to more than one million percent annually! No wonder a large portion of the Venezuelan population has fled to refuge in neighboring countries.

Less dramatic has been the growing number of economies that are transitioning from socialism to emerging market economy status. These are economies that had been heavily controlled by central authorities and found themselves falling behind. They were not able to deliver to their populations the standard of living and promise that could be seen in market-based economies outside their borders. They also were riddled with corruption.

To better achieve their potential, these economies have adopted market-based principles and, in many cases, have experienced a take-off. Among these economies are China, India, Indonesia, Argentina, Vietnam, much of Africa, and the former Soviet-bloc countries in Eastern Europe. Notable are those in Africa, which, at the time of their independence, conflated capitalism with the colonial system they had struggled to throw off. They chose, instead, to adopt socialism, and, only after experiencing a growing list of disappointments, did they begin turning to market systems.

More than fifty countries, with over half the world's population, fall into the emerging market category. For political leaders, this has been a mixed blessing. They have been losing political control as reliance on decentralized markets has expanded, but the standard of living of their populations has turned noticeably better.

Some proponents of socialism have acknowledged that the historical record of socialism has not been very favorable. But they argue that the socialist systems up until now haven't been properly established and many of the shortcomings can be overcome by better design. Or they argue that they intend to follow the lead of the Scandinavian countries. However, as will be discussed in Chapter 5, the Scandinavians regard themselves as competitive market economies with extensive safety nets for their people—mature welfare states.

The discussion in this chapter suggests that any socialist system will be plagued by inefficiencies leading to a smaller pie available to be shared among its members. In addition, they will experience more sluggish growth and less improvement in the well-being of their citizens. Furthermore, the greater involvement of the state in economic decisions throughout the economy will limit individual liberty and provide more opportunities for control of daily lives, as well as more scope for corruption by public officials. Despite protests to the contrary, socialist systems limit personal choice and are a threat to liberty.

SUMMING UP

- For many, socialist economies appear attractive at an abstract level. There's less cutthroat competition, more security, and perhaps a greater sense of togetherness. However, at a practical level, they're plagued by a plethora of difficulties. Blueprints for setting up and operating such a system are skimpy, at best.

- Some advocates of socialism point to the Bible for support. However, this is a very weak argument. The few passages that they cite provide very limited support. Moreover, socialist systems have been characterized by pervasive corruption and the Bible doesn't mince words in condemning corruption. To be sure, the Bible is clear in underscoring the need to care for the poor. But this is expressed as an individual or Christian community responsibility, rather than one assigned to government. The Bible is clear that charity is to be done willfully—not coercively—and cheerfully.

- Any economy faces a multitude of decisions. These are made on a highly decentralized basis in a market economy by individuals and businesses pursuing their self-interest. In a socialist system, the decisions have to be made by central planners having much less information than is available to the many participants in a market economy. Moreover, the complexity of those decisions expands exponentially as the economy develops.

- As a consequence, it's hard for a socialist system to match the ability of a market economy to produce goods and services. The coordinating role of the Invisible Hand, based on self-interest, isn't utilized. Indeed, socialist economies routinely have lagged their market economy counterparts—and the gaps keep growing.

- Nonetheless, some would argue that much of that greater volume of goods and services in a market economy is misdirected. Though it reflects choices of individuals—consumer sovereignty—it is argued that people don't make the best decisions for themselves. Whether a socialist system would do better in providing for the well-being of individuals depends on one's belief about whether a central planner can and **will** make better choices for people or whether that central planner will get sidetracked by other considerations.

- A socialist economy might be more successful in achieving broad distribution goals. But even if there were a consensus about what those goals are, a questionable proposition, there are innumerable decisions that need to be made by the central planners about when it's acceptable or desirable to have departures from full equality. For example, do those who perform more strenuous and less desirable work deserve more compensation, and do unhealthy people deserve more health care (especially if their poor health reflects their own lifestyle decisions)?

- Further contributing to the difficulties of a socialist economy are the lack of incentives for workers and managers to make decisions that benefit the public at large. Notable among these is whether there are sufficient rewards for managers to respond constructively to ongoing changes in the economic environment and innovators to want to make valuable improvements in products and production processes.

- Beyond these are incentives for abuse of power and for corruption as government is given more control over the lives of individuals. Moreover, inevitable mistakes and waste are likely to be perpetuated.

- The actual experience with socialism has been anything but favorable. Venezuela has been a debacle of disastrous human proportions. Less dramatic have been other socialist experiments, many of which have been abandoned and refocused on becoming emerging market economies. A surprisingly large portion of the world has chosen this course of action.

QUESTIONS FOR THE DINNER TABLE

1. Have your views on socialism changed from reading this chapter? If so, how have they changed?
2. What, in practice, is equality in the distribution of income? Are socialist systems able to achieve such equality?
3. Does socialism impinge on personal freedom? Is this good or bad?
4. What's meant by the statement that socialist systems short-circuit the role of the Invisible Hand? Is this good or bad?

CHAPTER 4

Communism and Fascism

BACKGROUND

Ironically, both communism and fascism (including Nazism) have described themselves as forms of socialism, although in the minds of many they're considered to be polar opposites. Moreover, some see an unbridled market-based—capitalist— economy as a cousin to a fascist economy. However, about the only thing that they have in common is private ownership of property.

Both communism and fascism are linked to controversial ideologies. As a consequence, both stir up strong emotions.

As noted, communist and fascist systems differ importantly on private ownership of property. In a fascist system, much of the property used in production of goods and services is privately owned. But, unlike a market-based system, producers in a fascist system don't have much control over their property and what and how much they produce. Under communism, property is collectively (state) owned. In both, a state-planning agency plays a key role in directing production.

Communism has seen itself as a global movement and, thus, tends to be outwardly focused. It seeks an international alliance or comradeship of workers. In contrast, fascism is nationalistic and inwardly focused and sees the nation state as the ultimate entity. It looks with suspicion on those outside its borders. Moreover, German Nazism viewed the German people to be a super (Aryan) race. It viewed the responsibility of the German government to preserve this race in its purest form.

COMMUNISM

Socioeconomic principles. Communism is linked to Karl Marx and his writings in the ***Communist Manifesto*** (1848) and ***Das Kapital*** (1867). He frequently collaborated with a friend and colleague, Friedrich Engels. Around the mid-1800s, a group of radicals had been promoting communism as a form of socialism, and Marx acted as spokesman and brought coherence to the thinking of the group. In his writings, Marx provided the intellectual underpinnings for this movement.[29]

---

29 In 1871, a group of workers took over Paris and this became known as the Paris Commune. It resembled the Paris commune that had been established during the French Revolution, roughly three-fourths of a century earlier. This commune served as an inspiration to Marx, who saw this as a first wave of workers taking action to overthrow the existing order.

Marx saw the prevailing capitalist system as having an inherent bitter class conflict between the owners of capital (capitalists or bourgeoisie) and their workers. Indeed, he viewed this in the context of Hegelian dialectic: workers (the proletariat) would rise up against their capitalist oppressors and seize control.[30] This would usher in an end to private property and introduce a dictatorship of the proletariat, which would be a prelude to a classless communist utopia. The communist utopia would be characterized by "From each according to his abilities, to each according to his needs." During the transition to this classless communist paradise, human nature would be fundamentally transformed from being self-focused (greed) to being focused on the greater good for the community as a whole.

The clash between workers and capitalists. Marx argued that there were inexorable laws of history. Each social system (thesis) through history had inherent conflicts (antithesis), which led to that social system being displaced and replaced by a new one (synthesis). During this process, the capitalist system replaced the feudal system. But the process comes to an end when the capitalist system is overthrown and replaced by communism. The final stage of this evolutionary process is communism, which doesn't contain such internal contradictions.

Marx's close collaborator, Friedrich Engels, labeled this the dictatorship of the proletariat, a phrase that was to be used by Lenin in Russia nearly a half century later.

30 This Hegelian dialectical was called dialectical materialism or, in abbreviated form, "diamat." Marx and his followers maintained that economic materialism was a major force driving historical events and was key to harmony in communist utopia.

Marx developed an economic model that was used to analyze the workings of the capitalist system. At the center of his model was the labor theory of value, in which he argued that the economic value of an item was determined solely by its labor content. Thus, the working class was responsible for creating all economic value. However, capitalists owned the means of production (factories) and employed workers.[31] They had leverage over workers, which they used to expropriate some of the returns from the effort of workers—so-called surplus value. Assisting them was a reserve army of the unemployed. These unemployed, in effect, kept employed workers from pressuring their employers to provide the full compensation that they deserved for the fruits of their labor.

The reserve army was created by greater mechanization of production that displaced workers and was a part of capitalists ever accumulating capital (such as manufacturing facilities) with the surplus value they were extracting from their workers. But returns from investing were seen by Marx to be ever diminishing, and capitalists responded by pushing and exploiting their workers even more to make up for the declining returns.

Meanwhile, capitalist systems were facing business cycles—booms and busts—of increasing intensity. These were being caused by a growing impoverishment of workers, which limited their ability to buy the goods produced by capitalists.

---

31 To complicate matters somewhat, the capital owned by the capitalist class was embodied labor— labor stored up during the production of the capital—and the returns to owners of capital were merely returns to stored up labor. The capitalists received these returns, although the returns actually belonged to the workers who produced the capital and had not been compensated fully for their efforts.

Overproduction developed because capitalists couldn't sell all that they produced to exploited workers, who didn't have sufficient means to buy it all.

The final throes of capitalism and the path to communist utopia. In response to greater swings in production and immiseration, workers (the proletariat) would be driven to revolt against this system, topple it, and take it over. Marx and Engels stated, "Let the ruling classes tremble at a communist revolution. The proletarians have nothing to lose but their chains. They have a world to win. Working men of all countries, Unite!"

The leaders of the proletariat would end private ownership of property and establish the dictatorship of the proletariat. This new regime would manage the transition to communist utopia, which may require helping people lose their acquisitiveness and penchant for private property. For those having difficulty making this transformation, they become candidates for a rehabilitation camp (gulag). Those who were especially intransigent might disappear permanently.

Because the problems with capitalist systems were seen to be widespread among the nations, the coming age of communism was seen to be universal, stretching across national borders (as suggested in the above quote by Marx and Engels). In this idyllic communist world, there would be no need for nation states and the conflicts that they produced would finally come to an end.[32]

---

32 Indeed, the movement of communists and other socialists developed its own anthem, *The Internationale. The Internationale* was to capture a global unifying theme and inspire workers around the world to rise up against the oppressive capitalist system they were under and to impose the new classless order. Its first verse and chorus are: "Stand up, damned of the

Communism and Biblical Teachings. Apart from the example in Acts 4—the isolated example of a temporary communal system—there's very little in the Bible that supports the argument for a communist system.[33] Indeed, Marx's collaborator, Engels, said, "If some few passages of the Bible may be favorable to Communism, the general spirit of its doctrines is, nevertheless, opposed to it." After all, as we noted in Chapter 2, Jesus said that the poor would always be with us until the millennial kingdom arrived. Utopia won't be achieved in this fallen world and will have to await the second coming of Jesus.

The communist movement has deemed itself atheistic. Marx said that religion was the "opium of the people." It served the interest of the capitalists by giving the oppressed workers a palliative in the form of the hope of a millennial kingdom. This hope would act to forestall the onset of the inevitable revolution. This enabled the exploited masses to cope with the economic injustice that they were experiencing in ever-heavier doses. Marx and Marxists have sought to destroy not only religion and private ownership of property but also the traditional family.

---

earth. Stand up, prisoners of starvation. Reason thunders in its volcano. This is the eruption of the end. Of the past, let us make a clean slate. Enslaved masses, stand up, stand up. The world is about to change its foundation. We are nothing, let us be all. This is the final struggle. Let us group together, and tomorrow the *Internationale* will be the human race."

33   The similarity between the statement in Acts 4 that "It was distributed to each as any had need" and Marx's statement that in communist utopia it would be "From each according to his abilities to each according to his needs" is probably more than a coincidence. Marx, as a boy, attended a Lutheran church in his native Germany, even though he was ethnically Jewish. He was baptized, and likely was captivated by the biblical passage while in the church.

Loyal communists needed to trust the ideological claims that utopia—the promised land—was just around the corner and there would be no need for religion. Moreover, the Judeo-Christian religion maintains that the claims of God on a follower are to take priority over other claims on the individual—including those of the communist movement. Permitting the practice of religion would compromise the full commitment needed for the communist revolution to be fully successful.

Liberation theology. Despite the seeming incompatibility between orthodox communism and biblical teaching, a movement has developed that's known as liberation theology. It has notably involved Catholic priests in Latin America and has embraced Marxist concepts. Capitalism is seen to be an evil and sinful system. It needs to be overthrown—even by violence— if it cannot be overthrown by other means. Particularly, capitalism impoverishes the masses and the call on the Christian is to confront this injustice. This becomes the primary way to bring the kingdom of God to this fallen world. Liberation theology relies heavily on Marxist teachings and tactics in organizing a social movement. Liberation theology has been criticized for viewing sin in the context of economic and social systems, rather than in the context of individual decisions to disobey God. Often, leaders in this movement have allowed Marxist ideology to dominate biblical teachings. It also deserves mention that the capitalist system that liberation theologians rail against isn't really a market-based economy but rather a ruling oligarchy that owns massive amounts of property. There have been a number of countries in the Western Hemisphere that have been targeted by liberation theologians. In most of these, the property was obtained through corrupt practices and was protected by the coercive power of the state. It's hard to argue that these places are not plagued by injustice.

The record of communism. The experience with communism has been anything but utopian. It began in 1917 with the Russian revolution and the formation of the Soviet Union. Later, in 1949, the Chinese communist party took control of Mainland China. Other Marxist systems were imposed on North Korea, Vietnam, Laos, and Cuba. Communism was adopted in some other parts of the world during the twentieth century, but by the end of that century only five formally remained—China, Vietnam, Cuba, North Korea, and Laos.[34] The more successful of these, China and Vietnam, have been reforming their economies by allowing private property and market principles to propel their economies forward.

Overall, the record of economic performance of communist economies has been abysmal, despite the claims of Marxism. The inherent inefficiencies of these systems and the heavy emphasis on building a strong military led to a low and stagnant standard of living for ordinary citizens. Communist systems replace the Invisible Hand—coordination of production through prices and the pursuit of self-interest— with cumbersome bureaucratic central direction. Notably, agricultural production has been especially paltry when collectivist farming has been imposed, often leading to the need for massive imports of food from

---

34 Other places where communism was imposed include Eastern Europe as satellites of the Soviet Union, Angola, Mozambique, Ethiopia, and Mongolia.

prosperous market-based economies to avoid widespread hunger. Farming was done in collectives that lacked the incentives to produce much and adapt as farming methods in other parts of the world were improving. Workers in factories, too, lacked incentives and were notoriously unproductive. Indeed, in the face of worker apathy, communist leaders commissioned artists to create murals and posters to inspire and exhort workers to work hard and produce more—what became known as great socialist art. Working hard for the collective came to be portrayed in public places as heroic.

Outside the defense sector, the quality of manufactured goods produced in communist systems has been uniformly shabby. Manufacturing has been performed by state-owned monopolies and the managers of these enterprises have had very little flexibility, and often operate under incentives that conflict with efficiency. The systems that distribute products to the public have typically been very unwieldy, often requiring the buyer to wait through long lines for each product that they buy. Product imbalances have been pervasive, with some items severely in short supply while others are in overabundance and pile up in warehouses. Over time, it became more and more evident that the standard of living of the citizens in these regimes was falling in relation to market economies. This contributed to the collapse of the Soviet Union and to a decided move toward market-based economies in China and Vietnam.

Another area where performance has been disastrous is the environment. Communist nations have amassed the worst records of environmental degradation. Moreover, the leaders of these nations have been unwilling to acknowledge the problem or accept assistance in dealing with it. Perhaps the worst environmental disaster in history was the Chernobyl nuclear disaster in the Soviet Union during the 1980s; at least 4,000 people died from exposure to radiation and thousands of others suffered from illnesses stemming from exposure. It's especially ironic that communist systems have such poor environmental records because critics of capitalist (market-based) systems argue that such capitalist systems inherently cause more environmental damage.

Politically, communist nations are one-party systems. After all, they're based on there being only one true ideology and, thus, there's no need for other parties espousing false, alternative claims. The Communist party represents the workers, those who ultimately prevail according to the laws of history. Moreover, communism is a classless system. Therefore, there are no other groups that need representation. To some, this is the purest form of democracy—the party is fully in tune with the desires of the masses and represents those interests fully. Those working for the state and executing orders issued by the state are necessarily representing "the people." "The people" becomes an abstraction and takes precedence over the rights and well-being of any individual.[35] Whatever the state decides is more important

---

35 I experienced this a number of years ago in a major communist country. I was waiting to cross the intersection of two major streets, which was governed by a traffic light. As the traffic light that I was facing was turning from red to green, a massive, state-owned dump truck, painted in military green, stormed toward the traffic light that was turning red. As the light was changing, I stepped down from the curb, expecting that the big truck would stop and I could proceed to cross the street in front of the truck—a fairly normal practice in the United States and other Western countries. But when I realized that the truck's driver was doing the people's business and that was deemed to require running the red light, even if it involved

than the well-being of any single individual—a very different perspective than that of Western democracies.

Interestingly, the most important leader in communist systems traditionally has been the secretary of the Communist party. This is because the system is based fully on Marxist ideology and the party is the keeper of that ideology, with the party's secretary being the final arbiter on issues involving ideology.

Communist systems have been characterized by very little personal freedom. If the party-driven government is acting in the best interest of the population at large ("the people"), individuals need only follow the directives of their leaders. Moreover, there should be no need for criticism because infallible leaders pursuing the directives of pure ideology will always be acting in the interest of the people. Furthermore, for a time at least, there will invariably be obstinate objectors who refuse to conform to the thinking and behavior required of good communists. In these cases, the prescription is "rehabilitation" in the form of retraining camps (gulags). Eventually, even these misfits will come to appreciate this new world and choose to conform and enjoy the utopia that has been given to them. If not, they'll rot in or mysteriously disappear from these camps.

In practice, there are inevitably going to be failures of the system, especially on the economic side, and there are powerful incentives to suppress the evidence. After all, how can a system

---

flattening me in the process, I quickly jumped back on the curb to avoid being a casualty. A single individual was clearly expendable in the conduct of the people's business. The locals, who had gathered on the curb to cross the street with me, had enough sense to stay on the curb until the truck passed, because they knew that they were of no significance compared to that truck.

that's transitioning to a utopian state based on the one true ideology make serious errors? Any person alleging such failures surely is disloyal—and even treasonous. Those doing so typically become enemies of the state and get charged with treason, punishable by consignment to prison camps or even death.

Viewed in this light, it may not come as a great surprise that perhaps as many as 100 million people have died at the hands of communist leaders over the past century. Individual human rights are greatly subordinate to the much more dominant cause of the movement. And, if you're unwilling to participate in the movement, there will be consequences and those consequences could be severe.

FASCISM

Economic underpinnings. Unlike communism, fascism doesn't have a very coherent ideology. The systems that developed in Fascist Italy and Nazi Germany saw themselves as a third way— highly distinct from both capitalism and Marxism. They held this view despite their leaders having been socialists or heavily influenced by socialist thinking. These systems were based on private ownership of property, but collectivist direction from the state—so-called corporatism. Like communism, the interests of the collective (the state) were to dominate those of individuals and businesses. In the words of Italian fascist dictator Benito Mussolini, "The citizen in the Fascist State is no longer a selfish individual who has the anti-social right of rebelling against any law of the Collectivity. The Fascist State with its corporate conception puts men and their possibilities into productive work and interprets for them the duties they have to fulfill." This is a pretty clear statement of where the rights of individuals rank in a fascist system.

Basically, the fascist state established monopolies of privately owned businesses and then directed them through a central planning agency. Trade unions representing workers were outlawed and workers councils under the direct control of the state were to represent the workers instead. These councils were to collaborate with corporate managers in furthering the aims of the state. There was to be a government-business partnership, so-called syndicates, with the government being the dominant partner. The government planning authority set prices. Thus, the natural working of prices in guiding resources and rationing scarce goods—following the direction of the Invisible Hand—was short-circuited. It was replaced by a clumsy central planning authority, comparable to those in communist systems. As a consequence, supply-demand imbalances were routine, resulting in shortages of some items and excess production of others. Moreover, unemployment was typically quite high. Not too surprisingly, the incentive to innovate by business managers and individuals also was blunted. Overall, fascist systems were plagued by waste.

Fascist systems established trade protectionist policies to limit dependence on the outside world. The goal was to achieve independence from other nations and thereby limit vulnerability to actions taken by other nations to cut off supplies coming from trade. Doing so meant that these nations were willing to forego the benefits from international trade. In trade, each party can gain by specializing in those areas where they have a comparative advantage and trade for those items that they don't have such an advantage.

Fascist systems tended to rely on public works programs focusing on infrastructure projects to absorb the unemployed. This played an important role because, as noted, errors in the economic planning process led to substantial amounts of unemployment. Public funds were used to hire the unemployed to build roads, bridges, and other infrastructure. The German autobahn system was built to serve this purpose.

In addition to directing production, fascist systems had some features aimed at redistribution. Thus, there were taxes on (and forced loans to be made from) excess earnings. Taxes were very high to cover the costs of a large military, public works, and other large public spending programs. However, considerable income inequality was tolerated, and loyalty to the regime carried substantial benefits. Moreover, differing social classes were also tolerated, if not encouraged.

Socio-political dimensions. As noted, fascist systems don't place value on personal liberty. Nor do they value democracy. Indeed, Mussolini viewed democracies as being weak and ineffective. Fascists viewed the state, in the right hands, as being able do a much better job than individuals acting collectively through the ballot box. This included the belief that they could better achieve social justice by overcoming the social and economic chaos that they believed inevitably accompanies democracies and market systems.

Fascist systems also have been highly nationalistic. Their leaders held the view that the citizens would be energized by a system that focused on glorifying the nation and the dominant ethnic group. Indeed, they initiated programs—pogroms—that removed the weaker and more dependent members of the society with the objective of engineering a genetically superior population. Hitler went much further by launching pogroms that were focused on exterminating certain groups—notably Jews, Gypsies, and homosexuals. Widespread medical experimentation was conducted using members of these groups as subjects without regard for the consequences for the person serving as a guinea pig.

In addition, fascist systems have tended to place military might as a high priority. They have seen themselves as entitled to the territories of neighboring nations and have built up a powerful military to conquer those places. World War II was caused by Nazi expansionism into neighboring nations.

Fascism and biblical teachings. It's hard to find any biblical support for fascism. The emphasis on ethnic and racial superiority flies in the face of biblical teachings that all persons are created in the image of God and are greatly and equally loved by God. As such, all persons have comparable dignity, regardless of background or ability. There's no hierarchy among peoples.

In fascism, the individual is clearly subordinate to the collective (state), and the collective has a stronger claim on the individual than God. Fascism is based on private ownership of property but state direction of the use of that property. As we have seen, the Bible seems to favor private ownership of property, but sees the owner as a steward of that property obligated to use the property responsibly in keeping with biblical teachings. Further, under fascism, there hasn't been much concern for caring for the poor. Indeed, the poor are viewed as being poor because they're weak and inferior. Thus, they can be disregarded or, even worse, exterminated.

SUMMING UP

- Both communist and fascist systems are linked to socialism. Both regard the individual as subordinate to the collective and both rely on central direction of the economy. In this regard, they both short circuit the workings of the Invisible Hand. In practice, they cannot replicate the results of a decentralized market process in which prices and self-interest play an essential role. They forego the utilization of information that comes about through the interlinking of multiple parties through the market.

- Communist and fascist systems differ in the ownership of property. Communist systems are based on collective (in practice, state) ownership, while fascist systems allow private ownership. However, property owners under fascism are highly restricted in how they use their property. They're subject to the dictates of the state.

- These systems also differ in that fascism is highly nationalistic while communism is universal in scope. Communism sees workers around the globe throwing off the shackles of capitalism wherever they may be. This is in keeping with the laws of history and part of the inexorable movement toward a communist utopia. Such a world will be characterized by a classless society and no need for national borders. In time, there will be no need for the state, and it will wither away. Heaven on earth has been ushered in.

- In practice, both systems have been brutal. They have led to the violent deaths of scores of millions of people.

- The views of many current-day socialists have an uncanny resemblance to those of fascism. They generally favor private property but argue that the use of private property is to be heavily controlled by government.

- It shouldn't be surprising that neither system has much of a foundation in the teachings of the Bible. This is especially true for the rights of the individual. The individual is subordinated to the collective. Allegiance to God first isn't something that can be tolerated. The ideologies of these systems promise utopia, but the Bible, in contrast, teaches that we'll continue to live in a fallen and imperfect world until Christ returns.

QUESTIONS FOR THE DINNER TABLE

1. What do communism and fascism have in common? How do they differ?

2. Communism has characterized itself as a global movement while fascism has been intensely nationalistic. What accounts for these differences?

3. Do you believe that communism and fascism are compatible with the teachings of the Bible? Why or why not?

4. Why do you think that these systems have been highly brutal in the past? Is this inevitable?

CHAPTER 5

The Welfare State

BACKGROUND

Over the past century, governments have extended their reach far beyond their traditional primary mandate of protecting citizens from harm, be it from inside or outside the country, and administering justice. Widespread has become the provision of housing assistance, health care, income in retirement, other income support, and education through the secondary level and beyond. In 2015, the size of government in relation to the economy (government outlays as a share of GDP) varied from 25 percent (Colombia) to 57 percent (Finland) for countries in Europe and the Americas. The United States is somewhere in the middle at 38 percent (federal, state, and local outlays in relation to GDP)). This is up sharply from a century earlier when the size of government in the United States was only about 7 percent of the overall economy. Much of the expansion took place at the federal level owing to New Deal policies during the Great Depression of the 1930s. At that time, the view emerged that the federal government should take a very active role in addressing problems occurring at the national level, relegating state and local governments to a backseat role. Beyond spending measures, governments have expanded their control over the economy by taking on a greatly expanded regulatory role, directing how businesses and individuals use the resources that they own.

The Scandinavian countries have what's widely believed to be the most extensive welfare state. These countries regard themselves to be competitive market economies, while providing cradle-to-grave benefits for their population. As noted later in this chapter, the Scandinavian countries extended their welfare programs to the point that their economies were suffocating under the yokes of those programs, but then backed off.

RATIONALE

Among the reasons for this expansion of government has been to provide for the less fortunate—having taxpayers provide the funds to government to distribute to the poor. In America, this has involved a proliferation of government programs. Programs provide public housing or housing subsidies to lower-income families. Other programs help with the purchase of food, provide health care, and cover childcare. This piecemeal approach—with a multiplicity of administrative costs—has been chosen over one that provides a cash payment to cover all these expenses. In large part, the piecemeal, targeted assistance is done to ensure that public funds are not diverted to unintended purposes, such as alcohol, illicit drugs, or fancy cars. Simply giving cash to low-income families to ensure that they can buy the essentials raises concern that recipients will squander the funds on other things. Interestingly, the poverty rate in the United States has not shown any distinct trend over the past four decades, despite a huge ramping up of spending to alleviate poverty.[36] The poverty rate has averaged a little less than 15 percent of the population—climbing in economic downturns and retracing those movements in economic expansions.

Another reason for expansion of government has been to socialize risk in certain areas of our lives. We don't know what the future holds, and we all face some types of risks that can have devastating consequences. For example, our homes can catch fire and be destroyed. For many, their home is their single largest investment and to lose it would have catastrophic consequences. For this reason, we buy insurance on our homes and other property having high value. The more valuable the property, the higher the premium for insurance. We also buy insurance on our lives to provide financial protection for our family members, in the event we should die unexpectedly. For these kinds of potential losses, we have relied on the private insurance market. Government gets involved through regulation of insurance providers.

---

36 The threshold for the poverty rate has been defined to be three times a nutritionally adequate diet for a family. This amounts to roughly $25,000 for a family of four. But, notably, the measure of income used to determine the poverty level excludes noncash assistance, such as Medicaid, food stamps, and housing assistance.

However, the private insurance market has proven to be problematic in some other situations. This is especially true for health insurance for people with preexisting conditions or for other reasons deemed to be a high risk by health insurers. A number of health insurers are willing to offer insurance against serious illnesses or injuries. However, the premium that they charge the individual is based on the expected cost of the claims that will be filed by that individual. For someone who is healthy and is unlikely to face a major illness, the premium will be low. However, for someone who is unhealthy or comes from a family plagued by health problems, the premium will be much higher. Moreover, for one who already has a serious illness (a preexisting condition, such as cancer), the premium will be still higher. Many view higher premiums for those already having or being vulnerable to serious illnesses to be unfair and want the government to do something about it. As a consequence, the government has increasingly gotten involved in the health care sector. Not only has health care policy been focused on such catastrophic situations, like those above, but it has also extended into routine care, such as visits to the doctor for hangnails, colds, or the flu.

Another form of publicly provided insurance is unemployment insurance. Here again, we're dealing with a situation—the loss of a job—that can create major difficulties for a family. So, the federal government has devised a program in which it collaborates with the states to help workers who lose their jobs. Still other government programs have been established to help those facing substantial losses from natural disasters, such as tornados, hurricanes, and floods, and, more recently, from losses coming from global pandemics.

Beyond these, the federal government has been heavily involved in retirement programs. Social security is the most notable. The objective behind social security was to ensure that people were setting aside sufficient amounts of funds during their working years to have a basic level of income and decent standard of living during retirement. People with jobs must contribute to social security during their working years, and, in return, are promised a schedule of benefits in retirement based on their contributions while working. However, the benefits promised have exceeded the contributions made by a typical worker. As a result, the payments to retirees are now running above the amount collected from workers, and the program will run out of funds in the 2030s, absent a large infusion of taxpayer monies. The federal government also provides healthcare in retirement through Medicare—in which employees are passed from employer-provided health care to the federal government—and provides tax subsidies for certain other retirement plans; the tax subsidies take the form of exemptions from paying taxes on earnings devoted to qualified pension plans.[37]

Thus, government has been providing an ever-expanding safety net to cover various adverse events. This is in addition to a wide array of assistance to those with low incomes. Moreover, there has been growing sentiment, especially among millennials and Gen Zers, for government to provide other services free of charge—such as higher education and health care. There's

---

37 The employee does not have to pay taxes on those earnings that are contributions to qualified retirement funds when the earnings are made. The employee does have to pay taxes on pension benefits when they are received. However, that is far in the future and often the retiree is in a lower tax bracket at the time.

also growing sentiment for government to provide a universal basic income—regular cash payments to everyone, with no strings attached.

BIBLICAL BASIS

It has been argued that Scripture—both Old and New Testaments— has mandates for government to provide for the less fortunate. For example, Psalm 72 (verse 2) says, "May he (the king) judge your people with righteousness, and your poor with justice!" It goes on (verse 4) to say, "May he (the king) defend the cause of the poor of the people, give deliverance to the children of the needy, and crush the oppressor!"

A passage in the New Testament that some see as justifying an active role for government in providing for citizens is Paul's instruction in Romans 13 (verses 3 and 4), "Then do what is good, and you will receive his (the ruler's) approval, for he is God's servant for your good."

These verses provide a clear injunction for governmental leaders to take measures to help the poor by addressing injustices against the poor. However, it would be a stretch to conclude that these verses prescribe that leaders should establish programs to provide a safety net, unless one regards income inequality to be an injustice—even if it's not caused by the rich taking advantage of the poor.[38]

---

38   It is interesting to recall the words of God to the prophet Samuel when the people were clamoring for a temporal leader—a king. He warned them that this governmental leader will engage in excesses and pay for this by imposing heavy taxes on the people. See 1 Samuel 8: 10-17.

However, we saw in Chapter 1 that the Bible is very clear in prescribing that it's the responsibility of individuals to help the poor. In other words, we as individuals have a personal responsibility to act as a safety net for the less fortunate, especially those unable to care for themselves. This can also take the form of a corporate effort through the church or other group in which those involved are participating voluntarily.[39]

Moreover, when we respond as individuals and churches to those in need, there's a personal connection that takes place between the giver(s) and the recipient. The recipient can feel the love of Christ as it's transmitted through the giver(s). In contrast, distribution becomes impersonal when we allow government to substitute and be the intermediary. Furthermore, it becomes much easier for the recipient to view the transfer as something that they're entitled to—and not come into contact with the one who has sacrificed on their behalf—and for the taxpayer who is compelled to contribute to public assistance to become resentful.

---

39 Jared Rosequist, in *How Would Christ Vote?* (Amazon, forthcoming), uses the account of Jesus feeding the 5,000 men and its aftermath in Chapter 6 of John to argue that Jesus was sending the message to those involved that they should not expect handouts, such as those promised by the welfare state. After feeding the large group from five loaves of bread and two fishes, some in the group came back for more handouts, but Jesus mentioned that they should be seeking the spiritual nourishment that He was offering instead. People who only get physical nourishment eventually die, but those receiving His spiritual nourishment enjoy eternal life.

IMPLICATIONS

Welfare state programs act to short-circuit the workings of the Invisible Hand and, thus, have implications for the utilization of productive resources. As such, they result in inefficiencies and shrinkage of the overall economic pie. Let us examine these effects.

When subsidies are provided, such as in free health care or free higher education, the demand for the item being subsidized expands and the supply contracts.[40] A shortage (excess demand) will be the result. That is, more will be demanded than is supplied. At this point, public policy has two basic options: develop a nonprice rationing mechanism for allocating the available (reduced) supply or develop a method for expanding supply to meet the greater demand.

Rationing. Rationing can be done in various ways. The most common method is to utilize first come-first served. Having people wait in line until the available supply is exhausted follows first come-first served. Those ending up later in line will be the ones who go without, regardless of how much they value the item being rationed in relation to those who were are able to get to the head of the line.[41] Creating a waiting list based on the order in

---

40   This is illustrated by Figure 4 in the appendix.

41   In these situations, there will be a trade opportunity in which unsatisfied demanders can offer to buy the item from those who had their demand fulfilled, provided the item can be transferred. This can work for tangible items but is more complicated for intangible services. Giveaways such as bobbleheads, often are used to attract spectators at athletic events, but the number of items given away is limited. Very often, some of the successful

which requests were made for the good or service being rationed, such as a visit to the doctor for an illness, follows the first come-first served method. This is practiced under the British health care system for a variety of situations and the waiting times can be very long, even for people with serious ailments.

A second method of rationing is to award the available supply based on chance, such as a lottery. While this may be seen by many to be fair, it's unlikely that those getting awards will be those valuing and needing the item the most.

Another rationing method is to establish criteria for deciding those deemed to be most worthy to receive the rationed item. This is practiced widely in higher education where prices to students are set well below the market-clearing outcome and there's a perpetual excess demand at the more prestigious schools. In these cases, test scores, previous academic performance, having alums in the family, and various other criteria are used to determine selections.[42] Of course, going to free education would result in a greater degree of excess demand and the extent to which such criteria would need to be used would intensify.

Rationing can also be achieved by having a review panel make the decisions. For example, a medical review board can be established to determine who gets treatment for life-threatening illnesses. The board might consist of government employees,

---

spectators put the item up for sale on venues such as eBay and those who value the item most highly in this way have an opportunity to acquire it.

42 The college admittance scandal of 2019 illustrates the extent to which parents will go to get their sons or daughters into elite schools—including bribes in the hundreds of thousands of dollars. This is another example of how excess demand invites corruption.

medical professionals, or a mix of both and perhaps others.[43] In many cases, they will be making life and death decisions. Interesting examples are the cases of toddlers Charlie Gard and Alfie Evans in the United Kingdom. Both little boys were under the care of hospitals that were part of the British health service— the nationalized ("free") health care system in the United Kingdom. In each case, the doctors at the hospitals treating the boys determined that the boys had incurable illnesses and should be cut off from life support. They decided that scarce treatments should be directed to others, despite feverish pleas from both sets of parents. Moreover, both sets of parents had lined up experimental treatments–one in the United States and the other in Italy—at no cost to the health service. However, the courts denied the parents the opportunity to leave the country for potentially life-saving treatment for their sons—an eerie example of what can happen when the state has the final say in life and death situations, even in an advanced, civilized nation.

Of course, corruption can be an effective method for allocating available supply. Indeed, bribery has been the most common method of dealing with excess demand over the centuries and is widely practiced today. With bribery, public officials who control the decision of who gets the item in short supply make the decision based on the one who is willing to offer the most in under-the-table payments. The bribe can take

---

43 Note that a review panel will absorb resources that can be used elsewhere to create value. If the review board is composed of health care professionals, these professionals will not be able to provide the same amount of health care as if they focused on health care full time. Relying more on the price mechanism allows allocation decisions to be made in the course of price determination, which frees up these resources to provide more health care.

the form of a cash payment or it can be more subtle, such as an offer to provide home improvements to the official in charge or to provide that person with a free vacation.

The Bible is very clear in condemning bribery and corruption. Moreover, corruption offends greatly the sensibilities of people everywhere. Deep public disgust over widespread corruption has frequently been the driving force behind popular protests and uprisings aimed at cleaning up or overthrowing corrupt governments.

Augmenting supply. The other option is to develop a method for augmenting supply—so that supply expands to match the greater demand. Using regular economic incentives to induce more supply implies that the remuneration offered to the producers of the good or service in short supply will need to increase. That will result in a higher cost per unit.

Before the item was subsidized, the lower-cost suppliers had already responded to meet the former (lower) amount demanded. But at a reduced or zero price, more will be demanded, and to get more production, higher-cost suppliers must be drawn in to bring forth more production. Costs will rise because new, higher-cost producers must be paid enough to make it worth their while to enter this arena. On top of this, it's almost inevitable that compensation received by those already producing the item will rise in tandem, further boosting cost.[44]

---

44 It's tempting to hold down overall cost by just paying the new suppliers enough to get them to produce more and to continue paying the original suppliers the same as before. However, it's difficult to discriminate in paying new suppliers more than others. For example, existing producers can reconstitute themselves as new producers in order to get higher

Governments typically respond to increases in such costs by trying to limit payments to all suppliers. For example, the Medicaid program in the United States provides health care free of charge to lower-income individuals and puts a cap on payments to health care providers. Enabling some people to get health care at no cost to them has substantially added to the overall demand for health care. In response, this has placed additional pressure on the cost of health care, including costs to the government.

The government has attempted to hold down these increases by imposing a schedule of maximum fees to be paid to health care providers for services provided to Medicaid recipients. But for many providers, the limited Medicaid payment is insufficient for them to be willing to treat Medicaid patients. As a result, roughly half of all physicians in urban areas have chosen not to participate in Medicaid, and this has curtailed the quantity and quality of health care available to lower-income persons.[45] The Medicaid example illustrates that there are substantial consequences from efforts to expand supply and, at the same time, hold down the increase in costs.

---

payments or there may be rules against paying some differently than others. The end result is that the government will be incurring a huge new cost to meet all the demand. This can be seen in Figure 4 in the appendix.

45 Were the government to compel health care professionals to accept Medicaid patients at the government-set rate, many current health care providers would choose to withdraw from their profession and many prospective providers would be less inclined to enter the health care field. The consequence would be fewer resources in the health care sector instead of more. Of course, the government could direct (force) people to be health care providers, but this would come at the cost of a huge loss of personal freedom.

VA HEALTH CARE

A good example of an excess demand situation and the problems that are caused is the Veterans Administration (VA) health care system. Roughly 40 percent of the 23 million military veterans are enrolled in the VA. Health care is provided to them by this federal agency. Patients don't have much latitude for selecting their health care provider; their provider is assigned to them. It's what's called a single-payer system. Veterans are not charged for their VA health care and there are ceilings on salaries of VA health care workers and ceilings on other payments, including to drug suppliers. These are intended to contain overall costs.

This structure acts to reduce supply from what it would be in a regular market setting, while the absence of charges to health care users results in more demand for health care than in a regular market setting. The outcome is excess demand for VA health care. In other words, there are chronic shortages.

In recent years, more public attention has been directed to VA health care, especially long wait times and substandard quality. The VA attempts to prioritize access to available supplies by placing enrollees into eight separate categories, with disabled veterans being placed in the higher categories and getting priority for health care. Those in the lower categories are subject to longer wait times.

In response to revelations of long wait times and shoddy health care for veterans, the program has been changed to allow patients to get care from private providers. This move to augment the supply of health care provided to veterans is adding to the overall cost of the program, in keeping with the point made in the text.

Interestingly, VA health care participation varies over the business cycle—increasing with unemployment during recessions and decreasing with improving employment opportunities during expansions. As the economy improves, unemployed veterans find jobs with health care benefits. In these circumstances, they opt for privately provided health care through their employers. This is a pretty clear statement about the quality of VA health care compared to what's available in the private sector.

The VA health care system is a good example of what to expect if those who favor a single provider system in the United States (so-called "Medicare for everyone") are successful. Chronic shortages would become commonplace, and a method for deciding who gets priority treatment would need to be developed. Patients would have little choice regarding their health care provider, unless a private sector health care system option were permitted and those choosing this option paid the full costs of their privately received health care.[46]

Welfare programs. As noted, a multiplicity of public programs are available at the federal, state, and local level to help the

---

46 Some advocates of a single-payer system have argued that patients would still be able to choose their doctor. However, this is not very realistic. Patients would be seeking the better-known doctors with better reputations, leading to more demand for them than for other providers—and a serious imbalance would occur. Some doctors would end up with more patients than they can handle, while others would have very few. In order to avoid charges of favoritism or other unfair measures for assigning patients to doctors, it is likely that a random process would be used for assigning patients to doctors—with patient choice being a casualty.

poor. These include Medicaid, mentioned above. Also on the list are subsidies for housing, public housing projects, food stamps (Supplemental Nutrition Assistance Program or SNAP), child-care programs, and various others. All have significant administrative costs. Approximately 125 separate programs have an annual cost that exceeds $1 trillion. The administrative costs of these programs total about $50 billion annually. These numbers imply that government programs for the poor spend an average of $22,000 for each person in poverty or $88,000 for a family of four. This translates to an average cost of $3,000 that must be paid by each and every American in the form of taxes.

Viewed from the perspective of the distribution of income, the average income of households in the lowest one-fifth of the population in the United States was $20,000 in 2015 before taxes and certain transfer payments, Medicaid, disability, and SNAP (food stamps). When adjusted to include these transfer payments, average income for this group rose to $33,000—a 65 percent increase.[47] Adjusting income to include other transfers would boost this figure significantly more.

In contrast, households in the top one-fifth averaged $292,000 before taxes and transfers and after they had $215,000—more than a 25 percent reduction. These figures indicate that currently there's a significant amount of income transfer from upper to lower income households through federal government programs. There's even more redistribution when state and local programs are included.

---

47   "The Distribution of Household Income, 2016," Congressional Budget Office, July 9, 2019.

Notable has been the tendency for the poverty rate to be stuck just below 15 percent of the population, despite the many programs aimed at getting it lower. Contributing importantly to this stagnation has been virtually no progress in closing the education gap between those with low incomes and others. This points to a need to strengthen the education provided to those in low-income groups, which implies radical new approaches to educating our children; just tinkering with the long-prevailing approach won't do the job.

It's also important to note that these anti-poverty programs discourage work, unless the benefits are tied to willingness to work.[48] As we noted in Chapter 1, the Bible is fairly clear in regarding work to be something that's good for a person. It gives people a sense of dignity and provides them with an opportunity to use their God-given talents to solve problems that help others. Furthermore, there's a widespread view that public programs that induce beneficiaries to work less while taxing those who work are wrong and unfair. Beyond this, providing assistance to those who don't work or choose to work minimally can be seductive for them, and can induce them to choose a lifestyle for which the rewards from gainful employment are not experienced. And this can trap subsequent generations into doing the same.[49]

---

48 One of the more robust results in economic research is the so-called income effect on the willingness to work. Leisure (the absence of work) is considered to be an economic good for which people want more as their economic means expands (their income increases). In other words, they want to work less as they can afford more leisure, which these programs foster.

49 A program that is targeted for the poor and tends to encourage more work is the Earned Income Tax Credit (EITC). The EITC augments earned

Universal Basic Income. Growing in popularity around the globe is the idea of a government-provided Universal Basic Income (UBI), which would provide all families with a basic level of income. The amount would vary with the number of dependents and would be provided to all, including the wealthy. Such a program would eliminate the administrative costs of the proliferation of government public assistance programs. Moreover, the UBI would reduce many current distortions that lead to misallocations of resources. Currently, the recipients of the various subsidized items are induced to utilize more of them than they would if they received the same amount of the subsidy in cash instead.[50]

However, the UBI would weaken the willingness to work. This would be true not only for the poor—those currently receiving assistance—but for all others as well. As noted elsewhere, this type of seduction to leave the workforce ultimately undermines one's sense of fulfillment and self-worth.

Moreover, it would be extremely costly. For example, if each American were to be provided $22,000—the average amount currently provided to people covered by government

---

income with tax credits as eligible persons earn more, up to a point. This provides an incentive to work more. However, the subsidy gets phased out as the recipient's income increases, which reverses the incentive to work.

50   Economic principles and evidence are very clear: When an item is subsidized, such as housing, people receiving the subsidy are induced to consume (utilize) more of the subsidized item than they would if they received an amount of cash that is equivalent to the subsidy. In other words, if they received the cash, they would use that cash to consume (utilize) more housing (but not as much as when it is subsidized) and more of the other items that they want. That is, they tend to over-utilize the subsidized item in the sense that they value the additional housing that they receive at an amount below the true, underlying cost of providing it.

poverty programs in the United States—the annual cost to the government would be more that $5 trillion. This is $4 trillion more than currently being spent. Federal government outlays would more than double, even if the UBI were to replace all current federal spending on the poor. Moreover, it would come at a time when the federal government is grappling with a widening shortfall of taxes from outlays—a deficit outlook that already is out of control and unsustainable.

The unsustainable federal budget is being driven by entitlement programs—mostly promises for health care and retirement (social security)—that have proven to be much more costly than originally projected. Actually, the assumptions on which these programs were established have proven to be much too optimistic, and the costs of these programs have been compounded by extending them to more and more groups. These choices were politically expedient at the time by proponents—the view being that any difficulties in paying for them will have to be dealt with by others down the road. Baby boomers entering their retirement years and becoming eligible for social security and Medicare are exposing the flaws in the structure of these entitlements.

Adding more entitlements, such as free health care for all or a UBI, would place a burden on future generations that would be onerous at best. Greece has already tried this—an example that will be discussed later in this chapter—and the consequences have been extremely painful.

Guaranteed employment. Also gaining traction are proposals to guarantee a federal job for people who cannot find acceptable employment elsewhere. This would resemble the massive public works program developed in the United States in the 1930s in response to pervasive unemployment and in Nazi Germany to deal with those unemployed as a result of that nation's misguided national socialist policies.

Government would need to find some kind of work for those who enrolled, even though there would often be a skills mismatch between the worker and the job. It would place a sizable burden on federal agencies to find meaningful work for those opting for a federal job. And, if a federal job is guaranteed, what measures would be available for dealing with recalcitrant workers who refuse to do assigned jobs? Could such workers actually be terminated for not performing? Governments have been notoriously constrained in their ability to deal with underperforming employees.

Moreover, there would be inevitable pressure to boost compensation for these workers, since the government, of all employers, should be paying its workers well and setting a good example for other employers. This would add more to the costs of the program. Furthermore, as the government pays more, more people will opt for federal employment instead of private-sector employment. Private-sector employers would need to respond by raising wages, which would lead to higher costs and prices for the goods and services that they sell.

Paying for it. Paying for such large public programs—be they for poverty reduction or for other purposes—ultimately boils down to higher taxes, primarily on income.[51] And higher taxes

---

51   It has been suggested that we could borrow more funds to cover larger outlays and deficits. However, this has features of a Ponzi scheme, in which the cost is shifted from one generation to the next. At some point,

have economic consequences. Taxes discourage people from pursuing better economic opportunities and discourage risk-taking. As a consequence, the size of the economic pie shrinks.

The evidence shows that countries that provide large welfare programs sacrifice performance. Indeed, the Nordic countries have some of the most generous public assistance programs and some of the highest taxes to finance them. The programs get expanded to the point that they stifle the economy and compound the tax burden. Then they tend to go through a political cycle that results in reformers getting elected to streamline and roll back welfare-state programs when the public is chafing at the steep cost of these programs. They revolt against not only the high taxes that they must pay but also the adverse effects on their standard of living and on the willingness of able-bodied people to work.

A living wage. Another idea that's getting support these days is the idea of requiring employers to pay a "living wage"—one that enables workers to have an acceptable standard of living.

---

investors in Treasury securities (the lenders) will go on strike. They will refuse to acquire more federal debt unless they have assurances that the fiscal house is being put in order, or they will treat U.S. government securities as junk bonds requiring much higher interest rates to cover the risk of default. Alternatively, some have argued that we can inflate our way out of this mess using expansionary Federal Reserve monetary policy. However, such a course of action would only cause interest rates to jump much higher to compensate investors for the greater erosion of purchasing power caused by inflation and lead to soaring interest costs for the Treasury. Meanwhile, inflation would undermine the underlying workings of the economy and, as a consequence, the ability of the economy to generate tax revenue would be impaired.

In other words, the proposal is to boost the existing minimum wage substantially. Some cities, such as Seattle, have gone ahead on their own to raise the minimum wage that must be paid by employers in their jurisdiction.

Will this solve the problem of poverty in the United States if it's applied nationally? Economic principles and evidence clearly indicate that it will help some—but at the expense of others.[52] Employers are willing to pay workers for what they contribute to the business. When they're required to pay a higher wage, some workers—those who are not sufficiently productive—will find themselves in a position in which their contribution falls short of what they must now be paid. They will be released from their employers and will face a huge uphill battle finding work elsewhere. In other words, the most vulnerable employees will be the first to go. Moreover, as automation (including application of robotics) takes on more tasks and moves up the job skill ladder, the scope grows for these vulnerable workers to lose their jobs and to face difficulties in finding others. Those losing jobs then become the responsibility of the government's safety net.

Who are the most vulnerable workers? They're typically those with the least (and poorest) education and least on-the-job experience. This, unfortunately, falls heavily on minority teenagers.[53] Furthermore, when jobs dry up for these individuals, the opportunity to get critical job experience dries up, too—a Catch 22 situation in which feelings of self-worth tend to be

---

52   See The Effects on Employment and Family Income of Increasing the Federal Minimum Wage, Congressional Budget Office, July 2019.

53   The unemployment rate for African American teenagers is about five times greater than for the population as a whole and nearly double that of white teenagers.

dragged lower. Thus, raising wages in this manner comes at a considerable social cost.

Programs that improve the productivity of the more vulnerable workers are much more effective. These include solid basic education, technical education, and on-the-job training programs. When designed and implemented carefully, education and on-the-job training can do much more than other approaches in helping marginalized members of the workforce become productive and contented members of the population.

CHALLENGES FACED BY WELFARE STATES

As noted above, the United States is now confronting the difficulties of paying for a welfare state that was built on overpromises. Nonetheless, there currently is a political movement for adding considerably more to the welfare state. We can look at the experience of Greece and that of the Nordic countries to get a better picture of what lies ahead. These are largely market-based economies that have built large welfare states.

Greece over decades built an unsustainable welfare state. Particularly notable was Greece's extremely generous retirement system, especially for employees of the large government sector. Men were able to retire as early as age fifty-eight and women as early as age fifty. For police and military, full retirement was available to people in their mid-forties. Moreover, in many cases, pension benefits could be passed along to offspring. Beyond this, all workers were allowed two months of vacation, including two weeks at both Christmas and Easter. This added substantially to labor costs, made Greece uncompetitive in the global market, and lowered employment, while adding to the number of people collecting government assistance for being unemployed. As a consequence, Greece as a nation was consuming far more than it produced, and this was manifest in a large fiscal deficit of the national government. Borrowing from outside Greece made up the difference.

This lasted for quite some time, until private-sector lenders backed off as they realized their chances of being repaid were vanishing quickly. Once private creditors (lenders) backed away, Greece turned to fellow national governments and international institutions for lending assistance to avoid the pain of bringing their standard of living into alignment with their more limited capacity. In return for outside assistance, Greece had to roll back entitlements substantially, sparking vitriolic protests in the streets daily. Unfortunately, government cutbacks took place at a time when the country was already in recession—a time which called for fiscal stimulus instead of fiscal contraction to stabilize the Greek macroeconomy. The unemployment rate in Greece reached nearly 30 percent at its worst and has drifted down to a still massive 18 percent. Much of this acute pain could have been avoided by bringing entitlements into alignment with reality much sooner.

In contrast to Greece, the Nordic countries have scaled back their welfare states once they realized that their outlook had similarities to that of Greece. These nations have been known for their cradle-to-grave welfare systems. But it first should be recognized that each of these countries relies heavily on markets for guiding production and employment. They also tend to culturally be more homogeneous than most other nations; thus, there's less disagreement regarding public policies. While offering an extended hand to the less well off, these cultures place a high value on individual responsibility, including the importance of work. Over the decades, these nations have extended their welfare-state programs, which has placed strains on their national budgets, discouraged work effort on the part of the primary beneficiaries, and restrained economic growth. Notably, when these countries have come to realize the unsustainability of their welfare-state programs and the undesirable outcomes of staying on that path, they have opted for reforms that trim welfare-state programs back. As a consequence, they have been able to avoid the tragedy of Greece. We won't have to wait too much longer to know whether American leaders will come to a similar realization.

SUMMING UP

- The biblical argument for the welfare state isn't very strong, not nearly as compelling as the charge for individuals to act on their own accord (and through voluntary corporate efforts, such as through churches) to care for those in need. Nonetheless, the trend has been to expand the role of government in providing for the less fortunate and in socializing certain types of risk, such as adverse health situations.

- Many government programs are intended to make health care or other services available at low or no cost. These result in excess demands for those items, requiring a system of nonprice rationing or a scheme for augmenting supply to meet the greater demand. The latter approach adds considerably to costs and causes other complications.

- Also, welfare programs tend to discourage recipients from wanting to work, which doesn't square with biblical teaching about the value of work. Furthermore, the expanding welfare state has been acting to blunt the role of the Invisible Hand in guiding resources in the economy.

- Ironically, the poverty rate has not declined much as the government has expanded programs for the poor. Moreover, these programs have tended to discourage recipients from working, entrapping generations into a lifestyle of dependency. It's hard to avoid the conclusion that these programs are not having their intended effects.

- The ideas of a Universal Basic Income and living wage have gained in popularity in recent years. The former leads to reduced incentives to work for all of the population while the latter has adverse effects on some of the most vulnerable members of the population.

- The costs of the welfare state are substantial, not only in the form of higher taxes but also in terms of a smaller economic pie and less growth.

- It also needs to be recognized that as government extends its reach into ever-expanding corners of people's lives, the opportunities for corruption and abuse expand exponentially. Moreover, as people transfer more decisions regarding their personal lives, they're simultaneously handing over personal freedoms.

QUESTIONS FOR THE DINNER TABLE

1. Do you think that the welfare state is compatible with the teachings of the Bible?

2. What's the best way to care for the poor in keeping with biblical commands? What government programs might be most effective in providing for the poor?

3. Do you consider the Scandinavian nations to be good examples of socialism or the welfare state? Who owns property in those nations? Who decides what gets produced?

4. Is further expansion of welfare-state programs likely to impinge on personal freedom? If so, how?

Epilogue

For many, socialism seems to have a feel-good sense, offering security in a time great uncertainty, and seems to be loosely connected to biblical values. But, as we've seen, it's hard to find much biblical support for the foundational pillars of socialism—especially collective ownership of property and centralized decision making. As a consequence, it seems highly unlikely that Jesus would pat the advocates of socialism on the back for advancing their brand of socialism.

Instead, we can find more support for the underpinnings of a market-based system—private ownership of property and decision making at the individual level. Moreover, instead of chaos resulting from the disparate actions of so many economic units participating individually in a market system, there actually is an underlying order. Prices and markets coordinate the actions of all these parties and utilize all the information held by each of them. This becomes even more important as the number of parties involved and the complexities of production processes expand, including across borders. Furthermore, the end result in a competitive marketplace will tend to be high quality products at low prices reflecting costs of production. And the workings of this process ensure that these costs are minimized.

Such a favorable outcome occurs as individuals, in their capacity of consumers, workers, and businesses, pursue their self-interest. As Adam Smith noted about two-and-a-half centuries ago, it's as if there's an Invisible Hand coordinating the multitude of actions of all these entities into something that benefits the common good. It's noteworthy that Adam Smith was a follower of Christ—inspired by Scripture—and labeled himself as a moral philosopher (not a worldly economist). He saw order emerging from what seemed to be chaos. Market systems also have something akin to a natural mechanism for correcting mistakes promptly. Looking at the system as a whole, market economies have a counterpart in the order that occurs in the natural realm—the cosmos and lifeforms on earth—that reflects the work of an intelligent designer.

However, market systems have their flaws, which isn't too surprising in a fallen world. Included among these is poverty—some members of society are unable to provide for themselves through participation in the economy. Some lack the ability to provide for themselves, while others have been dealt a tragic loss that has put them in a deep hole. In these circumstances, the Bible is very clear that others have an obligation to step in and help out. Indeed, Adam Smith argued that we are created with a concern for the well-being of others, in addition to a desire to pursue our self-interest. This prompts us to respond to the needs of others and is reinforced by ample biblical instruction. However, biblical teachings focus more on a voluntary individual or group responsibility rather than a government responsibility for responding to the needs of others. Deferring to the state for this provision is a rather passive way of responding to a biblical calling, and one that precludes a personal connection between donor and recipient.

Other areas of market shortcomings are environmental degradation. This occurs when the costs of actions that lead to environmental deterioration are not borne fully by the perpetrators. But there are well-established ways that we can use public policy to achieve better outcomes. And the results have been pretty impressive. In contrast, the environmental record of centrally directed economies has been disastrous.

Income inequality has also been listed as a serious shortcoming of market-based systems. While statistical measures tend to overstate the degree of inequality, many are not equipped to meet the skills qualifications for good jobs today. Inequality isn't confined to market economies. Socialist systems have had their own problems of inequality.

It's also noteworthy that in a market system, the consumer is "sovereign." The choices of individuals in the marketplace determine what gets produced. A similar notion applies to individual voters in a democracy. They determine their leaders and the way they are to be governed. Both can be traced back to the Enlightenment period, which, in turn, goes back to the Protestant Reformation. They derive from natural human desires to be free and from natural law, both installed by the Creator.

Socialism, and its communist and fascist cousins, forego the workings of markets and prices in coordinating production. As such, they replace the Invisible Hand with centralized planning and centralized direction of the economy. This commonly leads to serious imbalances in the economy, as the price mechanism isn't utilized to bring supply into alignment with demand. Moreover, these systems also short-circuit incentives to introduce new and better products and to seek to produce all products more efficiently. The incentives for creativity are damped in the process, and with it the internal satisfaction that comes from creating something new or better. As a consequence, the standard of living for their populations tends to stagnate, even as they attempt to copy improvements achieved by market systems. At the same time, these systems don't eliminate inequality. The privileged, in practice, use their influence to ensure that they and their families get better treatment. Moreover, with the state involved to a much greater extent in economic life, there's much more scope for favoritism (corruption) to prevail.

Communist and fascist systems are based on ideology. This makes it very difficult to admit to the inevitable mistakes that will be made by the central planning mechanism. After all, if the ideology embodies truth, then how can ideology-based decisions result in mistakes? They then use the powerful state apparatus to suppress knowledge of these errors and eliminate anyone who might not play along.

These systems also subordinate the individual to the collective. As a consequence, individuals who don't go along with the will of the state are often treated harshly. Indeed, these systems have willfully exterminated large numbers of their populations.

As noted, another consideration is the extent of corruption. A popular conception is that market-based economies are plagued by corruption; businesses are seen to bribe other businesses to get contracts and to bribe public officials. It should be clear from the discussion in this book that the scope for abuse expands with the involvement of government in the economy. In a market economy, sound business practices and public disclosure rules result in a substantial amount of transparency and limit the opportunity for abuse. But when abuse takes place and is revealed, markets tend to punish the offending businesses severely.

In market-based economies, the size of the government sector has grown substantially over the past century. These economies have become, in varying degrees, welfare states. Much of this growth has taken the form of providing for the poor and socializing certain types of risk. Moreover, there has been growing sentiment for governments to go further by providing to everyone free health care and higher education, a Universal Basic Income (UBI), and impose a living wage. Some have argued that these kinds of government programs have a biblical basis, although it's hard to find much in the Bible that calls for the government to address these areas apart from rectifying injustices.

Programs by governments that offer services free or at highly subsidized prices invariably lead to shortages or carry with them huge costs. Moreover, public assistance programs tend to discourage recipients from seeking work—and the Bible views work to be good. Furthermore, these recipients can be seduced to become permanently dependent on public assistance. Despite more programs and resources devoted to eliminating poverty, the poverty rate in the United States has been relatively stable for decades.

A more straightforward and effective approach to reducing poverty and inequality is to increase the productivity of those at the lower end of the income scale. This can be achieved through various measures: better formal education, more and better technical education, and more support for on-the-job programs that enhance job skills. Certainly, improving the formal education system will require major reforms and the time for those reforms is long overdue.

In sum, Jesus can be expected to tell socialists such as Bernie and AOC that they're taking the wrong path for tackling serious problems. Personal (and voluntary cooperative) effort and not government effort to help those in need will prove to be more successful. Yes, wealth can be a problem, especially when greed has a grip. But this happens when one's wealth takes on more prominence than God. Also, be careful about coming up with solutions that discourage personal initiative and work. Work is fulfilling as is the application of God-given creativity for solving problems. These are brought out by the pursuit of self-interest in a market economy, in keeping with God's intelligent design. Finally, realize that striving to make improvements in the lot of others is highly commendable, but saving their souls from an eternity apart from God is vastly more important. Utopia needs to await the second coming, and that's reserved for those who have accepted the free gift of grace.

Drilling Down: Principles for Evaluating Economic Systems

INTRODUCTION

The tools of economics are very useful for some issues but quite limited for others. Efficiency and equity are typically thought to be the primary goals of an economic system. Very often, they're in conflict—policies that are intended to improve equity come at the cost of efficiency. This was seen in the discussion of the welfare state in Chapter 5.

Those economic tools are extremely helpful in evaluating matters relating to efficiency but have limited value in addressing issues involving equity. Moreover, as we'll see, equity is a more nebulous concept. Nonetheless, the tools of economics can be used to assess the cost of improving equity and to evaluate the efficacy of alternative ways of achieving certain goals regarding equity.

It's widely thought that market-based systems result in more inequality in the distribution of income. But, as we'll see, much of this inequality stems from factors that most would regard as legitimate, such as age (older people have more experience and are more productive than their younger counterparts, who someday will be in a similar position). And experience with collectivist systems has demonstrated that some persons—such as public officials, prized scientists and athletes—are given demonstrably more than others, such as better apartments, cars, and nice vacations. So much for equality in those systems.

The terms "wealth" and "income" tend to be used interchangeably by many. While related, wealth and income are different concepts. Wealth refers to the amount of assets one owns (minus total indebtedness). Income refers to how much one earns over a period of time, such as a year. Economists call the former a stock and the latter a flow. For example, if you have a savings account, the balance in the account corresponds to the stock (a component of one's wealth) and the interest you earn on the account is the flow (a component of one's income). People acquire wealth by saving out of their income, by appreciation in asset values (such as a rise in the price of a stock one owns), or from gifts, such as inheritances. For the bulk of the population, the primary component of their income is their labor earnings.

It's worth noting that there's a life cycle of income and wealth. Earnings grow over the working life of a person, owing to improvements in their productivity. This derives from experience on the job, from formal training programs, and from having newer and better equipment and software to work with. Wealth also grows over time as savings accumulate and as certain asset classes—such as stock and home prices—experience price appreciation. While wealth and income usually are highly correlated, it's possible for someone to have a high income, but little wealth. This would be the case if one earned a lot but spent (consumed) it all.

In the discussion of equity, differences in consumption are deemed to be important. One person has nicer clothes, a better car, and a better house, eats steak more often, and indulges in massages more than another person. Presumably, we care about differences in income and wealth because they lead to differences in consumption.

In this appendix, we'll first look at the issue of equity and then go on to develop some useful tools for examining efficiency. These can be applied to evaluate the alternative economic systems discussed in the text.

EQUITY

For some, equity is achieved when all have the same income or consumption. But this raises various questions. Does this apply across the board to all items? Should a person who is 250 pounds get the same amount of food daily as one who is 120 pounds? What if the heavier person isn't any taller, but is obese? Or should they have the same income or budget and be able to decide how much to allocate toward food and how much toward other things? Is it permissible for a person to sacrifice spending today in order to be able to spend more in the future, in which case there will be different levels of consumption today and in the future? These are difficult issues to sort out and opinions are going to vary.

Moreover, there are reasons why incomes vary that most would regard as legitimate. First, some people work longer and harder than others. Second, some people spend more time in school and in training for a job (including on-the-job training), and, as a consequence, they're more productive. Third, some are more careful in minding their health and are able to show up for work more regularly and are more productive when they're on the job. Fourth, some jobs are less pleasant or involve inconvenient hours. For example, few people are inclined to clean up a bar after closing—including cleaning toilets, emptying ashtrays, and mopping floors after 2 a.m. These less-appealing jobs usually command a premium.

Fifth, some lines of work entail more risk. For example, an entrepreneur may set up a bicycle shop in an as yet undeveloped area outside a city, counting on growth of residents with an interest in biking to make the venture worthwhile. If the guess is correct, then people moving into that community will have the benefit of a convenient bike shop and the entrepreneur will be rewarded with good earnings. If the guess were wrong, the entrepreneur would be scraping to make ends meet. It's the nature of risk–taking that one can win big or lose big. Most people are averse to taking on risk and must be compensated for risk taking.

Sixth, as already noted, age makes a difference. People who are older tend to be more productive than those who are younger in their line of work. Seventh, and a little more controversial, some are born with greater talent (or stamina) than others. For example, LeBron James was gifted with exceptional physical stature and coordination for playing basketball, a sport that's followed widely by serious fans. As a result, he has an income that's in the stratosphere. Eighth, and also somewhat controversial, some parents give their children more attention than others, particularly fostering learning and development of skills that will be highly valued later on in the workplace. The result is that their children will fare better in the marketplace.

The factors above account for a considerable amount of differences in the distribution of income (or wealth). However, other factors tend to raise more eyebrows. Inheritance is one of those. Historically, those who've inherited great wealth have been viewed as benefitting solely from privilege. However, as noted in Chapter 1, God did provide rules for inheritance—property being passed from one generation to the next. Also, racial or other forms of discrimination have contributed to inequality. A large body of law has developed in the United States addressing many forms of discrimination. Even more important, the Bible doesn't condone such discrimination and views it to be sinful.

In practice, the distribution of both income and wealth in the United States is highly unequal and has grown more so over recent decades. For example, the top 1 percent of wealth holders own about 35 percent of all wealth, up from 30 percent a quarter century ago. The top 10 percent own 75 percent of all wealth, up from two-thirds a quarter century ago. The distribution of income isn't as skewed as that of wealth, for reasons that have already been mentioned: The age factor plays a bigger role in wealth because accumulated savings rise more rapidly with age than income. It's worth noting that the bulk of those who are in the upper income and wealth groups have made it on their own and haven't benefited from inherited wealth. Moreover, large accumulations of wealth don't stay in the family very long. They're usually dissipated over a couple generations.

Among the reasons for inequality are globalization and rapid technological change. Globalization is good for many but is detrimental to others. Those who pursue opportunities in sectors that benefit from trade with other parts of the world—such as finance and information and medical technology—benefit considerably. In contrast, those who are in sectors that have lost to other parts of the world languish, such as those in the clothing and furniture manufacturing sectors. Also, the payoff from higher education, especially in technical fields, has become greater over recent decades, implying that those who pursue careers requiring higher education are being rewarded well for their choice.

Technological change has been proceeding at a brisk pace. This is eliminating some—lower-skill— jobs while creating new, higher-skill opportunities. Those prepared for the new jobs do well while those getting pink slips are losers. In other words, those designing robotics products that do the tasks of workers are prospering while those being replaced by robotics are looking for work.

For many, the distribution of wealth and income is considered greatly in need of repair. Apart from saying that more redistribution is needed, few will say what the correct distribution should be. Is a minor peeling off from the rich to give to the poor all that's needed? Or should wealth (and income) be equalized across the board? Or is the right outcome somewhere in between?

And economics has little to contribute to the issue. Indeed, economic tools cannot tell us whether a dollar given to a poor person will improve that person's level of satisfaction more than it will improve the satisfaction of a rich person, even though our intuition tells us that it's better that the dollar be given to the poor.

Nonetheless, some economists hold the view that redistribution from rich to poor can be justified by the proposition that the contribution to one's sense of well-being (utility) of each additional dollar to one's wealth diminishes as one acquires more wealth (based on the so-called law of diminishing marginal utility believed to occur as one consumes more of a particular good or service, such as ice cream cones). This notion seems plausible. If one makes the additional assumption that a given amount of wealth contributes the same to each person's well-being (and the incremental contribution to well-being from each additional dollar of wealth is the same across individuals), then one can make the case that overall satisfaction (utility) is maximized by transferring wealth from rich to poor. Indeed, this logic argues that global utility is maximized through a full equalization of wealth.[54]

While this may be true, the tools of economics cannot confirm this result because interpersonal comparisons of utility cannot be made (there's no unique calibration of utility or satisfaction that can be compared across individuals). Moreover,

---

54   This logic follows the nineteenth century contributions of Jeremy Bentham and the so-called utilitarians. Bentham was a British philosopher who argued for policies that would create "the greatest good for the greatest number."

even if this were possible, should the goal of an economic system be an overall maximization of utility—a critical value judgment—or should it be something else? What if achieving this goal resulted in the curbing of human freedom? Or came at the expense of discouraging innovation that improves lives over time? How are these considerations to be weighed? As noted, the goal of equity isn't one that's easy to settle using the tools of economics.

In essence, the issue of equity is a normative issue that's based on value judgments. This applies primarily to the matter of income distribution. One may have strong views on what constitutes an appropriate distribution of income or wealth, but those views cannot be supported by economic principles. As noted in Chapter 1, the Bible doesn't prescribe equality and has a number of examples of God blessing obedient servants with substantial wealth.

EFFICIENCY

In contrast, economics has a lot to say about efficiency. By efficiency, we typically mean something along the lines of getting the most out of our resources. But this is about as helpful as achieving equity, discussed above. To come up with more meaningful conclusions, we can start with the concept of Pareto efficiency—introduced by a nineteenth century Italian economist and philosopher, Vilfredo Pareto. A Pareto-efficient measure is one for which at least one person is made better off without anyone else being made worse off. This seems pretty reasonable. However, it should be noted that the goal of efficiency is based on the value judgment that efficiency is good.

Consumer valuation. Now, let us explore what we mean by being better off. First of all, economics deals with the reality that we must make choices. We're confronted with choices because we don't have the wherewithal (income) to get all the goods and services we want. Therefore, we need to prioritize, and select those items that make the greatest contribution to our well-being (satisfaction), allowing for what we must give up to get them. Basically, we value a good or service by what we're willing to give up to get it. A market economy relies on the use of money for making purchases—general purchasing power. When buying goods and services, we commonly use the amount of money we're willing to pay for a unit of a good or service as representing the amount that this good or service contributes to our well-being. It stands to reason that the amount a person is willing to pay for an additional unit of a good depends on the amount consumed of that good, declining as the amount consumed increases.

This can be illustrated for an individual in Figure 1 below. Measured on the vertical axis is the amount that this individual is willing to pay (sacrifice other goods and services) for each unit of this item (jeans). This is the price and it's measured in terms of the monetary unit—in this case, dollars. On the horizontal axis is the quantity of this item consumed. Suppose that we're examining the demand for designer jeans by a single individual. Note that the amount the individual is willing to sacrifice for one more pair of jeans decreases as the quantity consumed increases. The first point shows that the individual is willing to pay as much as $100 for the first pair of jeans. The second one is valued less, and the individual is willing to pay $90 for that pair. The amount that the individual is willing to pay continues to diminish as more jeans are acquired. At some point, the amount the individual is willing to pay drops to zero (not shown). At this point, this person is saturated with jeans.

The line connecting all these points, **DD,** we call a demand curve or demand schedule. Now we have an objective standard for measuring the contribution of an item consumed to the economic well-being of this person.

FIGURE 1: DEMAND SCHEDULE

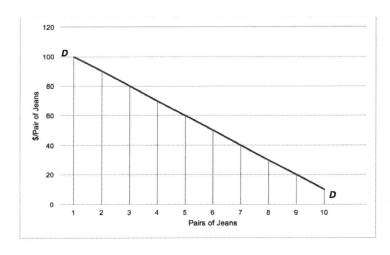

If one were to cumulate valuations across all individuals combined, it would entail summing each person's valuation schedule horizontally. For example, at a price of $80, we would tabulate the amount that each person would purchase and add them all up. That would be the quantity demanded in the market. The end result will be a negatively sloped schedule resembling the shape of the one above. Corresponding to the first unit of this good or service would be the highest valuation anyone places on the item (perhaps $100). Corresponding to the second unit will be the second highest valuation anyone places on this item (perhaps $95). This process would continue to the point at which the public is saturated with jeans, and the valuation placed on the last unit is zero. In the context of a market-based economy, the relationship between valuation and quantity is referred to as a market demand curve or demand schedule—an individual's demand curve represents an individual's incremental valuation of different quantities of the good or service, and the cumulative valuation schedule across all individuals is a market demand schedule.

Producer cost and supply. Another component of efficiency involves the amount that must be given up to produce a unit of a good or service. In other words, what's the value of other goods and services that must be foregone when a producer supplies a unit of this good? In our example of designer jeans, what's the value of other goods that can be produced with the denim, dye, thread, and so forth that goes into producing the pair of jeans? Once again, this can be measured in terms of the monetary unit. For example, the cost of producing the first pair of jeans might be $20, where this represents a comprehensive measure of costs (including the value of the time put in by the owner of the jeans factory).

It's the general nature of production processes that these incremental costs increase as the amount of the good produced increases. This is shown in the Figure 2, below. The first point illustrates that our producer can make up to 30 pairs of jeans at a cost of $20 each. That is, using the materials to produce the first 30 pairs would require sacrificing other goods and services valued at $20 for each pair produced. Note that the cost per unit rises as more jeans are produced. This occurs because producers utilize the easiest method for producing the first few units—pick the low-hanging fruit first—and then turn to the next easiest method (for, example, farmers farm their best land first and then their next-best second) and so forth. As larger quantities of inputs are needed to produce more goods, their productivity diminishes (the so-called law of diminishing returns). The result is more cost per unit and an upward-sloping supply schedule, as shown below.

FIGURE 2: SUPPLY SCHEDULE

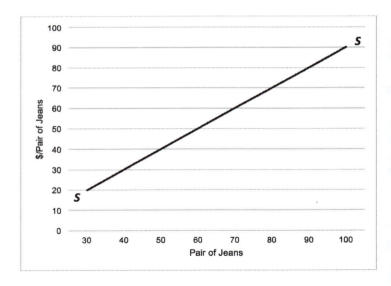

The relationship between the supply schedule of an individual producer and that of the market or collective supply schedule of all producers is similar to that between the valuation (demand) schedule of an individual and that of all individuals collectively. The market supply schedule is the horizontal sum of all producers' supply schedules. The first unit of collective supply is that of the lowest-cost producer of the first unit of output. The next amount supplied is that of the next lowest cost producer, and so forth. As a consequence, the market supply schedule entails incremental costs that increase as the quantity produced expands.

Optimal production and consumption. The optimal amount of the good to be produced and consumed is determined by the quantity at which demand matches supply. This is shown in Figure 3, below. Note that, in this chart, the demand and supply schedules are no longer individual demand and supply schedules. All consumers and all producers have been aggregated and this is reflected in a market demand and a market supply schedule, **DD** and **SS,** respectively. The optimal quantity occurs at the intersection of demand and supply—at a price of $50 per pair of jeans and an overall quantity of 2,000 pairs. At this point, the valuation of the last pair of jeans by consumers just matches the cost (value of other goods or services that must be foregone to get) of this last unit.

FIGURE 3: MARKET EQUILIBRIUM

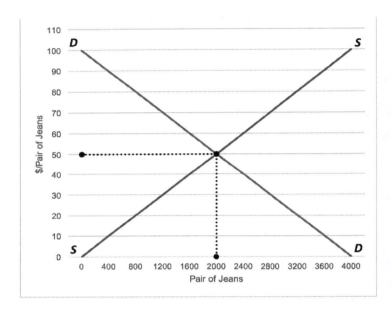

Anything short of 2,000 would mean that consumer valuation of an additional pair of jeans exceeds the cost of producing them (consumers would be willing to give up more than they have to). As it were, money would be left on the table. Production beyond 2,000 would mean that the value of the last unit consumed would fall short of the cost of that last unit. They would be better off by cutting back on this item and devoting the released resources to the production of other goods and services that they value more highly. Thus, 2,000 represents the point of maximum efficiency—the optimal amount. Note that at a market price of $50 per pair, each unit that consumers buy up to the last one is valued by them at more than $50. The excess of consumer valuation of each of these units over the price they pay ($50) is called "consumer surplus."

Competitive markets tend to give rise to this optimal outcome. Thus, market economies tend to be highly efficient. The Invisible Hand ensures this desirable result.

A subsidy. In Chapter 5, we discussed public policy of subsidizing some items, such as providing free health care (charging the consumer nothing irrespective of the actual cost of providing it). We can use supply and demand schedules to illustrate the implications. The schedules in Figure 4 below illustrate the demand and supply schedules, **DD** and **SS**, for visits to a health care provider. In a market setting, the equilibrium price would be determined by the intersection of the market demand and market supply schedules. The price per visit in this case would be $50 and the number of visits would be 1,800.

FIGURE 4: SUBSIDY

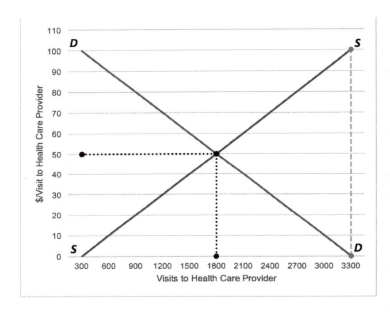

If the government established a program of providing free health care, the amount demanded would expand to the point at which the demand schedule intersected the horizontal axis (where the price is zero). This corresponds to 3,300 visits. At a price of zero, the supply would shrink to the point at which the supply schedule intersected the horizontal axis. This is point corresponds to 300 visits. The difference between these two amounts—that is, 3,300 – 300 = 3,000—would be excess demand. This represents the amount that must be rationed through one means or another described in Chapter 5. It could be rationed by first come-first served and long waiting lines, by a medical review board, or by some other means.

Alternatively, government could seek to meet all demand by drawing enough resources into the health care sector to expand supply to meet the amount demanded at a zero price, 3,300 visits. This would mean that suppliers would need to be paid an additional amount that would bring forth a willingness to provide 3,300 visits (moving up the supply schedule to point **S** at the end of the broken line on the right). This corresponds to paying health care providers $100 per visit, double what they were receiving under the original market situation.

In other words, the provider for each additional visit beyond the market-clearing quantity, 1,800 visits, requires compensation above $50. This amount continues to increase until it reaches $100 per visit to draw enough new resources to meet all demand at a price of zero. Those who had been in the health care business and had been willing to provide care at $50 per visit will find that they can charge higher prices for their services. In these circumstances, the total cost of providing free health care will soar.

Should the government attempt to contain the increase in cost by limiting payment per visit to providers, supply will fall short of demand. For example, if the government limited the payment per visit to providers to $50, the quantity of visits that providers would be willing to provide would be 1,800. This would fall well short of demand of 3,300 visits. Again, a means of rationing available supply would be needed. This is the situation confronted by the Medicaid and VA programs in the United States and by the National Health Service in the United Kingdom.

Other issues. Economic systems will differ along other dimensions as well. Notably, some will encourage more innovation than others. Innovation involves new or better products or lower cost methods of production. One way or another, it raises the standard of living of the population at large. Nonetheless, those being displaced by the accompanying change may be made worse off. Also, some economic systems provide individuals with more freedom to choose products to consume and the kind of work they do. While in others, these decisions are made by a centralized authority. This suggests that the value one places on personal freedom will be an important factor favoring one system over the others.

SUMMING UP

- Economics has limited tools for dealing with equity, notably the distribution of wealth and income.
- In contrast, economic tools are very useful in addressing the issue of efficiency.
- Pareto efficiency is a useful starting point: efficiency is improved by an action if the well-being of at least one person can be improved without anyone else being made worse off.
- From here, we can determine that the most efficient outcome occurs when the amount produced of a good or service matches the point at which the valuation placed on the last unit of that item just equals the cost of the item—the value of the other goods and services that must be foregone to be able to produce this item.

- In competitive markets, the optimal level of output is achieved.

- Policies intended to provide buyers with free or below-market prices will be characterized either by chronic shortages, requiring nonprice rationing, or substantial costs for being able to ensure that all demand is satisfied.

- Moreover, competitive economic systems spawn innovation and permit individuals a high degree of personal choice, both in what they consume and in their employment.

Acknowledgments

I wish to acknowledge the inspiration for this project that came from Corey Miller, president of Ratio Christi. Corey encouraged me to convert a talk that I had given to a Ratio Christi symposium into this book. I also want to thank Gary Williams, my SPS coach, for the guidance that he has provided in converting my manuscript into a final product, and to Wayne Purdin, who did an outstanding job in copyediting the manuscript. Both 100Covers.com and FormattedBooks.com did superb jobs in designing the cover and formatting the book, respectively, and working with them was a delight. In addition, I wish to express appreciation for the work of my colleague, Danny Soques, in creating the graphs in the appendix. Further, I want to thank Thomas Glatt for all the work he put into developing my website: Thomasdsimpson.com. Finally, I want to thank my wife, Cindy, for her encouragement and support.

Self-Publishing School

NOW IT'S YOUR TURN

Discover the EXACT 3-step blueprint you need to become a bestselling author in as little as 3 months.

Self-Publishing School helped me,
and now I want them to help you with this FREE
resource to begin outlining your book!
Even if you're busy, bad at writing, or don't know where to
start, you CAN write a bestseller and build your best life.
With tools and experience across a variety
of niches and professions,
Self-Publishing School is the only resource you
need to take your book to the finish line!

DON'T WAIT

Say "YES" to becoming a bestseller:
https://self-publishingschool.com/friend/

Follow the steps on the page to get a FREE resource to get started on your book and unlock a discount to get started with Self-Publishing School

Thomas D. Simpson is an economist who spent most of his career working on policy issues at the Federal Reserve Board in Washington, D.C. During this time, he provided technical assistance to several countries that were transitioning from socialist to market economies. Among these was primary responsibility for introducing a new currency in Iraq in 2003. In recent years, he has been a professor at the University of North

Carolina Wilmington (UNCW) and was an economic adviser to Dr. Ben Carson during his run for the U.S. presidency. Dr. Simpson also serves as the faculty adviser to the Ratio Christi chapter at UNCW. Dr. Simpson received his B.A. in economics from the University of Minnesota and his Ph.D. in economics from the University of Chicago.

You can learn more about Dr. Simpson by visiting:
Thomasdsimpson.com

CAN YOU HELP?

Thank You For Reading My Book!

I really appreciate all of your feedback, and
I love hearing what you have to say.
I need your input to make the next version of
this book and my future books better.
Please leave me an honest review on Amazon letting
me know what you thought of the book.

Thanks so much!
Tom Simpson

For a free workbook to assist you in getting
the most out this book, go to:
Thomasdsimpson.com/gift